Scamdemic: The COVID-19 Agenda

The left's plot to ~~win~~ steal the White House

by John Iovine

International Standard Book Number

ISBN: 978-1-62385-011-1

READ THIS FIRST – DISCLAIMER

The content and information contained in this book are for informational purposes only. The author, John Iovine, has narrated his research experiences in this book by observing and evaluating facts and figures. The reliance on the facts and figures has been done in good faith and believed to be reliable, according to the author's best knowledge. The sources of referenced information could change or be updated in the future. The author cannot guarantee the validity and accuracy of the sources, which may change, be modified, updated, or removed in the future, and thus, disclaims himself from any such changes, modifications, updates, and removals.

The information provided in this book is not and must not be taken as an alternative to any advice by a doctor, physician, or medical professional. If you know or suspect you have a health problem, you should seek your physician's advice. The readers should not use the information given in this book for diagnosing an illness or other health-related problems. Further, the readers also should not discontinue professional medical or health care advice because of something they have read in this book.

You should always consult with a medical doctor or professional health care specialist before using and relying on any data, information, or suggestion described in this book. Any reliance you make on any information presented in this book is at your sole discretion and risk. The author and publisher of this book hereby disclaim any liability for any medical outcome, directly or indirectly, in connection with the use of any information presented in this book.

"It's easier to fool people than to convince them that they have been fooled."

Quote by Mark Twain (allegedly)

Table of Contents

Chapter 1: Inconvenient Facts - Inside the Book

The legacy news media convinced the US population using the World Health Organization's misinformation that COVID-19 was 15X-20X more deadly than it is. State governors across the nation capitalized on people's fear to declare a "State of Emergency." That state of emergency gave the governor of the state complete authoritarian control to enforce unnecessary socioeconomic lockdowns. Lockdowns isolated, controlled and trained people into strict government obedience. Welcome to COVID-1984, the dystopian future we feared has arrived.

The state lockdowns suspended our constitutional rights and killed the booming U.S. economy. We were promised the lockdowns would only last a few weeks until we flattened the curve. The lockdowns continue even as the death rate from COVID-19 has flatlined across the nation. We flattened the curve months ago, but state governors refuse to release their economic stranglehold and restore our constitutional rights.

The pandemic provided the perfect excuse to institute massive unsecured mail-in voting in battleground states to cheat the 2020 presidential election.

This book features information and data from credible sources that were minimally reported or ignored because it didn't push the political media narrative. The fake news media either restricts, censors, or mocks the science and scientists that don't adhere to their alarmist narrative.

I am front-loading this book with information because more people will look at this book than buy it. Of course, I want you to buy the book, but I want you to have a few takeaway facts even if you don't.

Slanting the Truth 101

Experts disagree all the time. One expert says one thing, and the other expert says just the opposite. To be fair and balanced, the media should report what experts on both sides of an issue are saying. But that's not how the fake news mainstream media operated. The fake news media politicized their reporting by just reporting from experts that supported their COVID-19 hysteria. When data was retracted, as it was done quite often, it was ignored if the retracted information didn't fit the political "scaremongering" narrative. Experts in the legacy media were kept focused on worst-case scenarios.

If you think the opposing "experts" perhaps weren't credible sources, you would be incorrect. The experts voicing their opinions to avoid overreacting to the COVID-19 hysteria include the *New England Journal of Medicine*, Stanford University top epidemiologist Dr. John Ioannidis, and internationally, Sweden's top epidemiologist Anders Tegnell. In the end, these ignored experts were correct.

- The World Health Organization told the world that the mortality rate of COVID-19 was a whopping 3.4 % to 4.5 %. They then compared this to the mortality rate of the flu at 0.1%. This fearmongering misinformation was the primer for creating the fake pandemic. This WHO-derived mortality rate stated that thirty-four to forty-five people out of 1,000 would die from the COVID-19 virus—the actual mortality rate estimated by our CDC is less than 0.2 percent. (And this was before the Trump vaccine.)

  That is less than one-fifteenth to one-twentieth (1/15 to 1/20) of the fatality rate claimed by the World Health Organization of 3.4 % to 4.5 %.

  Source: [https://coronavirus.jhu.edu/data/mortality].

  Even this estimated mortality rate from the CDC is based on using wildly exaggerated COVID-19 death numbers in its calculation.

- All COVID-19 deaths are intentionally inflated. The CDC changed its standing seventeen-year reporting procedure for filling out death certificates to inflate the number of COVID-19 deaths. The new guidelines for COVID-19 changed the comorbidities procedure. Regardless of the cause of death, if a person tests positive for COVID-19, the death must be attributed to COVID-19. Fatal gunshot wounds to the head are not the cause of death if the person has a positive COVID-19 test, the CDC demands the death be listed as COVID-19.

- Had the CDC not changed its comorbidities procedure, it is estimated that reported COVID-19 deaths would be reduced by more than 90 percent. The CDC reports that only 6% of the reported COVID-19

Deaths are from COVID-19 alone. See Chapter 10 for more information.

> Table 1. Deaths involving coronavirus disease 2019 (COVID-19), Pneumonia, and influenza reported to NCHS by week ending date, United States. Week ending 2/1/2020 to 12/26/2020.*

Updated December 31, 2020

Week ending date in which the death occurred	All Deaths involving COVID-19 (U07.1)	Deaths from All Causes	Percent of Expected Deaths²	Deaths involving Pneumonia, with or without COVID-19, excluding influenza deaths (J12.0-J18.9)³	Deaths involving COVID-19 and Pneumonia, excluding Influenza (U07.1 and J12.0-J18.9)³	All Deaths involving Influenza, with or without COVID-19 or Pneumonia (J09-J11), includes COVID-19 or Pneumonia⁴	Deaths involving Pneumonia, Influenza, or COVID-19 (U07.1 or J09-J18.9)⁵
Total Deaths	303,823	2,913,144	112	286,866	139,982	6,949	456,580

The COVID-19 Death Number Reported by the Fake News Media

The number of COVID-19 Deaths, excluding Influenza - Not reported by Fake News Media. COVID-19 Deaths are exaggerated by doctors following CDC new Death Certificate Guidelines. See text.

Reference: [https://www.cdc.gov/nchs/nvss/vsrr/covid19/index.htm].

- The fake news media reports add influenza deaths to the COVID-19 deaths to inflate the total death numbers.

CDC States - Only 6% of the reported COVID-19 deaths are from COVID-19 by itself!

Comorbidities

Table 3 shows the types of health conditions and contributing causes mentioned in conjunction with deaths involving coronavirus disease 2019 (COVID-19). For 6% of the deaths, COVID-19 was the only cause mentioned. For deaths with conditions or causes in addition to COVID-19, on average, there were 2.6 additional conditions or causes per death. The number of deaths with each condition or cause is shown for all deaths and by age groups. For data on comorbidities, [Click here to download].

Source: [https://www.cdc.gov/nchs/nvss/vsrr/covid_weekly/index.htm].

6% of all reported COVID-19 (303,823) deaths are only 18,229 deaths. If we remove influenza deaths from that aggregated total, COVID-19 (139,982) deaths drop to just 8,399 deaths.

John Hopkins Reports Relatively No Additional Deaths in 2020 Due to COVID-19

On **Nov. 22, 2020**, John Hopkins published this truthful report. It created such a "liberal" furor that John Hopkins had to retract and delete the report from its website. **Another example of "Cancel Culture" intimidation and fact censoring.**

The data presented in the John Hopkins report appears to confirm that the amount of COVID-19 deaths did not increase the number of deaths in the United States as compared to prior years. Shocker! Had COVID-19 caused 300K plus fatalities, as the fake news media and their brainwashed zombie followers repeat ad nauseam, you would see this increase in the number of deaths in the United States, but you don't.

From the original John Hopkins report:

Surprisingly, the deaths of older people stayed the same before and after COVID-19. Since COVID-19 mainly affects the elderly, experts expected an increase in the percentage of deaths in older age groups. However, this increase is not seen from the CDC data. In fact, the percentages of deaths among all age groups remain relatively the same.

Transfer of Deaths

If you look at the death toll numbers for other causes of death, they all decreased in proportion to the deaths reported for COVID-19

From the original John Hopkins report:

> This trend is completely contrary to the pattern observed in all previous years. Interestingly, as depicted in the table below, the total decrease in deaths by other causes almost exactly equals the increase in deaths by COVID-19. This suggests, according to Briand, that the COVID-19 death toll is misleading. Briand believes that deaths due to heart diseases, respiratory diseases, influenza, and pneumonia may instead be recategorized as being due to COVID-19.

Source: [https://www.thegatewaypundit.com/2020/11/johns-hopkins-study-mysteriously-disappears-shows-spite-covid-no-deaths-2020-prior-years].

Source: [https://pjmedia.com/news-and-politics/matt-margolis/2020/11/27/johns-hopkins-study-saying-covid-19-has-relatively-no-effect-on-deaths-in-u-s-deleted-after-publication-n1178930].

Wayback Machine Link to Original Study Source:
[https://web.archive.org/web/20201126223119/https://www.jhunewsletter.com/article/2020/11/a-closer-look-at-u-s-deaths-due-to-covid-19].

The John Hopkins report appears to support the CDC's fact that only 6% of reported COVID-19 deaths are from COVID-19 by itself. If there aren't over 300,000 + excessive deaths in the US, there can't be an excess of 300,000 deaths due to COVID-19 as the liberal legacy media and their brainwashed followers continually repeat. There is a big difference between dying with COVID-19 and dying from COVID-19.

- **Still Closing Restaurants in December 2020**

  In December 2020, despite scientific evidence to the contrary, NYC Mayor Bill de Blasio and NY Gov. Andrew Cuomo had again outlawed indoor dining and threaten another complete lockdown. Why? For your safety! According to contact tracing published by the state of New York, restaurants and bars only account for 1.43% of COVID-19 transmissions.

Again, they ignore science and justify their ignorance by quoting the number of positive COVID-19 tests and cases. These COVID-19 positive tests have little to do with the number of active cases and little to do with the number of deaths.

Following is a chart showing the number of cases (green) and COVID-19 deaths (red). The CDC states that only 6% of the reported COVID-19 deaths (in RED) are from COVID-19 alone. The rest are comorbidities, like a fatal gunshot wound to the head, being reported as a COVID-19 death because of a positive COVID-19 test.

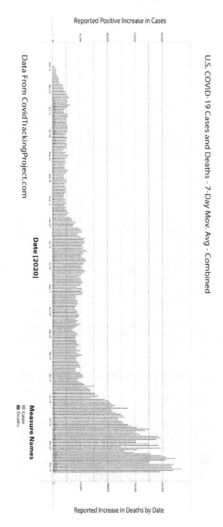

Every one of the millions of people who tested COVID-19 positive will be classified as a COVID-19 death if they die, regardless of cause.

Support Against the Scamdemic is Growing

- **Top Canadian Scientists Tells Government the Coronavirus is "The Greatest Hoax Ever Perpetrated on an Unsuspecting Public"**

  Source: [https://www.thegatewaypundit.com/2020/11/top-canadian-pathologist-tells-alberta-government-covid-greatest-hoax-ever-perpetrated-unsuspecting-public/].

- **Rand Paul stated the new lockdowns, "They're completely arbitrary."**

  Source: [https://www.theepochtimes.com/rand-paul-new-coronavirus-lockdowns-are-completely-arbitrary_3586096.html].

- **Rep. Jim Jordan Says Some COVID-19 Restrictions Have 'Gotten So Ridiculous'**

  Source: [https://www.theepochtimes.com/rep-jim-jordan-says-some-covid-19-restrictions-have-gotten-so-ridiculous_3590081.html].

- **Studies Prove Lockdowns Don't Control COVID-19**

  Source: [https://www.aier.org/article/lockdowns-do-not-control-the-coronavirus-the-evidence/].

  This is only one of the numerous studies that show lockdowns don't control the spread of COVID-19. But to keep the Scamdemic going, the media censored any study that doesn't promote the lockdown fallacy.

- **Democrats Want Continued Totalitarian Lockdowns Even After Vaccine.**

  President Trump has delivered on his promise to provide a vaccine for the China Virus within one year. As of mid-December 2020, the vaccine is being distributed across the country. To prove how democrats want to continue the totalitarian lockdown, they are floating talking heads on major news networks promoting continued lockdowns. NBC's Dr. Vin Gupta stated that people should restrict travel and continue to wear masks after being vaccinated.

- **Senator Ted Cruz (R-TX) responded on Twitter, "This is a bizarre, lunatic, totalitarian cult. It's not about vaccines or protecting people's lives — it is instead profoundly anti-science and is only focused on absolute govt control of every aspect of our lives."**

  Source: https://www.dailywire.com/news/nbc-doctor-masks-necessary-travel-restricted-even-after-vaccine?utm_campaign

- **Dec. 19, 2020 Deaths from Gunshot Wounds Still reported as COVID-19 Deaths**

  You may have thought this a joke when you first read that a gunshot wound to the head was reported as COVID-19 death. It was not, and it is still occurring across the country in every coroner's office. The government's mandate to inflate COVID-19 deaths force coroners to classify death by gunshot as COVID-19. Here is a December 2020 video from a Grand County Coroner:

  [https://www.air.tv/watch?v=lDm_pwxBQZyU5IRDf3eZKA].

  Source: [https://www.bizpacreview.com/2020/12/18/colorado-coroner-expresses-shock-over-inflated-covid-death-tallies-including-bodies-with-gunshots-1007116/].

- 80% of the people infected with COVID-19 do not get sick! They are asymptomatic, meaning they tested positive for COVID-19 and never knew they were infected because they had no symptoms.

  Source: [https://www.cnbc.com/2020/10/08/more-than-80percent-of-people-with-coronavirus-had-no-symptoms-uk-study.html].

  Source: [https://www.foxnews.com/health/coronavirus-asymptomatic-80-uk-study].

  Eighty percent (80%) of the people who do become symptomatic (get sick) with COVID-19 recover without any treatment or intervention or "spontaneously recover."

Source: [https://www.cnsnews.com/article/national/melanie-arter/dr-fauci-80-percent-coronavirus-patients-spontaneously-recover].

- **Facemask Sham** - Mandating face masks for healthy people is a sham. The *New England Journal of Medicine*, May 21, 2020: "We know that wearing a mask outside health care facilities offers little if any, protection from infection. In many cases, the desire for widespread masking is a reflexive reaction to anxiety over the pandemic."

  Source: [https://www.nejm.org/doi/full/10.1056/NEJMp2006372].

- **Social Distancing Sham** - Social distancing for healthy people, is another sham. Social distancing is pseudoscience extrapolated from a high school project from the George W. Bush administration. It was met with skepticism during the Bush administration when it was conceived. The CDC has no peer-reviewed studies because they do not exist. Social distancing is a pseudoscience.

- Fifty percent (50%) of all COVID-19 deaths are people over eighty-five years old. Only 8 percent of COVID-19 deaths are people under sixty-five years old.

- Hydroxychloroquine treatments cut the COVID-19 mortality rate in half. Instead of embracing hydroxychloroquine, information about its usefulness is censored, state governors restrict the drug's access, while doctors and pharmacies are being threatened if they prescribe or fill prescriptions. How many U.S. deaths by COVID-19 could have been saved if the fake news media did not attack the use of hydroxychloroquine? See Chapter 12 for the full story.

  Source: [https://thehill.com/policy/healthcare/505801-study-ties-hydroxychloroquine-use-to-lower-covid-19-death-rate].

- U.S. Population   329,227,746
  COVID-19 Cases   3,819,139 (July 21, 2020)
  COVID-19 Deaths*   55,719 (July 12, 2020)

What this information indicates is this:
1) Just over 1 percent of the U.S. population has been infected with COVID-19.**

2) You have a 98.54 percent survival rate if you become infected with COVID-19.

3) Only 0.016 percent of Americans have died from COVID-19, a 99.98 percent survival rate for Americans.

* COVID-19 Deaths excluding influenza deaths.
** Positive coronavirus antibodies may be caused by the common cold.

- In 2009 the CDC reported over 60,000,000 Americans were infected with the H1N1 virus. That's more than 15X the number of people "infected" with COVID-19. But you didn't see the fake news media and state governors going apeshit over that virus infection and case rate. The country wasn't forced into a lockdown. What's different? Who's the president is what's different!

  Source: [https://www.cdc.gov/flu/pandemic-resources/2009-h1n1-pandemic.html].

Beginning in 2021, Twitter will remove any tweets it considers misinformation about lockdowns, vaccines, or that COVID-19 (the China Virus) is not real or dangerous. I guess this book information will be censored off Twitter as well as Facebook.

Think for Yourself

I am not telling you what to think. I prefer you think for yourself. I am presenting information that has generally gone unreported by the mainstream media. This book is ladened with references to verify what I have written. I am not a doctor or medical expert; I report what doctors and medical experts have said.

1. If the way to stem a pandemic is to quarantine and treat the sick, why did U.S. government officials do the opposite and force a quarantine on most of the healthy population?

2. Why did Dr. Anthony Fauci and Dr. Deborah Birx, our top U.S. public health officials, "take for a fact" the unverified non-peer-reviewed ICL projection that 2.2 million Americans would perish? It was a projection by a scientist, Neil Ferguson, who historically provided incorrect infectious disease projections.

Chapter 2: The Coronavirus Con

Diamond Princess

I first heard of the coronavirus in relation to the *Diamond Princess* cruise ship. The ship was quarantined in early February 2020. The *Diamond Princess* provided an ideal petri dish environment for scientists to examine the COVID-19 infection and fatality rate. There were 3,700 people on board, 712 people tested positive, of which 567 were passengers and 145 were crew members.

Half of the people who tested positive for COVID-19 didn't have symptoms—that is 50 percent asymptomatic. Out of the infected people, thirteen eventually died. This appears to be a high fatality rate until you factor in the passengers' median age of fifty-eight. One-third of the passengers were seventy years old or older. Essentially this was a floating nursing home. None of the crew (who were younger than the passengers) perished. So, while it showed a high fatality rate, that fatality rate can be attributed to the passengers' age; we know the overall fatality rate of COVID-19 is less than 0.2 percent.

In February 2020, all the media were filled with hysterical predictions regarding this new, unknown coronavirus COVID-19. You would think the world was facing another black plague.

By the beginning of March 2020, I thought the U.S. was facing a viral apocalypse.

Hurricane Florence and the Fake News

Historically, the mainstream media oversells and dramatizes news, especially negative news. For example, when Hurricane Florence headed toward the U.S. coast in 2018, the mainstream news broadcast hourly progress reports. One reporter's live shot went viral. He showed himself struggling against the fury of the oncoming hurricane in South Carolina, digging his feet into the ground to steady himself against the onslaught of the "gale force" wind, yelling so his voice could be heard above the wind's noise. Unbeknownst to the reporter, residents calmly strolled behind the reporter during his dramatic live shot, unaffected by the hurricane winds. The reporter, not seeing the residents behind him, foolishly continued his dramatic struggle against the wind. And thus, the fake news was exposed.

I'm the guy walking behind the fake news reporting and exposing it.

When I decided to do my own research, the information I've uncovered was so contradictory to the promoted hysterical narrative; I started to write a few articles on the genuine threat the coronavirus posed.

This book began with those articles.

The conclusion I reached in early March 2020 was that the United States is in more danger from the hysteria being generated by the fake news mainstream media and politicians promoting the COVID-19 pandemic than by COVID-19 itself.

My opinion has never changed, although, at the time, I couldn't imagine the collateral damage the left-leaning fake news and Democrat politicians would willingly inflict on our country in their pursuit of power. I didn't imagine the out-of-control state governors using emergency powers to implement unconstitutional, draconian socioeconomic lockdowns, turning their states into banana republics with the governor as the *el Presidente*.

Since I am not a medical doctor or medical professional, you may be wondering how I knew it was a sham from the beginning. I started my research using only reliable sources, such as the *New England Journal of Medicine.*

New England Journal of Medicine

The *New England Journal of Medicine* released a report on February 28, 2020, regarding the danger from the COVID-19 coronavirus. One would think information from such a prestigious organization would be well-publicized in the media that was going hysterical with the coronavirus coverage; it was not.

The *NEJM* article didn't fit the fake news hysteria narrative, so it didn't make it to print. Meaning, it was ignored or covered so superficially, it may as well have been ignored.

So, what did the *NEJM* study report?

Data gathered from over a thousand coronavirus cases between December 2019 and January 2020 showed that the coronavirus appeared to be *no worse than the seasonal flu* with a fatality rate (they expected to be) less than 1 percent. Even that low estimate from the *NEJM* turned out to be high by a factor of three.

Source:
[https://www.nejm.org/doi/full/10.1056/NEJMoa2002032?query=RP].

The Centers for Disease Control estimated COVID-19 infection fatality rate is below 0.2 percent

The World Health Organization told the world that the mortality rate of COVID-19 was a whopping 3.4 % to 4.5 %. They then compared this to the mortality rate of the flu at 0.1%. This fearmongering misinformation was the primer for creating the fake pandemic. This WHO-derived mortality rate stated that thirty-four to forty-five people out of 1,000 would die from the COVID-19 virus—the actual mortality rate estimated by our CDC is less than 0.2 percent. (And this was before the Trump vaccine.)

That is less than one-fifteenth to one-twentieth (1/15 to 1/20) of the fatality rate claimed by the World Health Organization of 3.4 % to 4.5 %.

Source: [https://coronavirus.jhu.edu/data/mortality]

As of March 3, 2020, the coronavirus had only six fatalities in the United States. Even with only six deaths, the fake news mainstream media breathlessly reported and counted each new coronavirus infection and death. To keep the coronavirus crisis in perspective, last year, the CDC estimated 34,000 deaths in the U.S. due to influenza.

Flu = 61,000 Deaths (2017–2018) *
Flu = 34,000 Deaths (2018–2019)

Source: [https://www.cdc.gov/flu/about/burden/index.html].

- **Flu and Pneumonia = 177,000 Deaths (2017–2018)** The CDC estimated that approximately 177,000 people died in the 2017-2018 period due to the flu itself or by complications with pneumonia. These additional 100,000 people were not added to the flu deaths, with pneumonia as a comorbidity as is the case today with COVID-19. There were no lockdowns or mask mandates.

  Source: [https://nypost.com/2020/10/17/how-the-media-is-misreporting-covid-19s-death-toll-in-america/]

Coronaviruses are as Common as the Common Cold

The common cold is a coronavirus. Didn't hear that in the mainstream media hysteria, did you? So, the coronavirus has been around a while; it's the variant, COVID-19, that's new. If you become infected with COVID-19, the recovery rate is 98.57 percent.

Source: [https://www.webmd.com/lung/covid-recovery-overview#1].

Source: [https://www.usatoday.com/story/news/factcheck/2020/05/05/covid-19-fact-check-coronavirus-mortality-rate-misleading/3019503001/].

My mathematical analysis from July 2020 on the survival rate confirms the 98.57 percent survival rate.

My old Clorox wipes, manufactured before this crisis, clearly state the product kills the coronavirus.

Did you know that having had a cold can give you similar antibodies that will trigger a positive result for a COVID-19? It should make you wonder how accurate those COVID-19 antibody tests are, especially if they want to use those test results to force you into quarantine.

Elon Musk is recognized as one of the smartest men on the planet. He doesn't believe the COVID-19 tests are accurate. He had taken four tests in one day. Results? Two came back positive, and two came back negative.

Source: [https://nypost.com/2020/11/13/elon-musk-continues-to-cast-doubt-about-covid-19-test-results/].

We've Been Here Before—2009 H1N1

In 2009 the U.S. had a flu pandemic. It began in April 2009, and by October 2009, there were at least 20,000 cases and more than a thousand deaths in the U.S. before then-President Obama reacted and called a national emergency.

Source: [https://www.cnn.com/2009/HEALTH/10/24/h1n1.obama/index.html].

Could you imagine what the fake news media and socialist Democrats would say if President Trump waited until a thousand people died from COVID-19 before declaring a national emergency?

Dr. Fauci and the CDC under the Obama administration told the public that up to 40 percent of the American population might become infected with the H1N1 swine flu virus, resulting in 700,000 deaths over the next two years if a vaccine wasn't developed. The WHO declared up to two billion people worldwide could be infected.

The CDC reported over 60,000,000 Americans were infected with the H1N1 virus. That's more than 15X the number of people "infected" with COVID-19. But you didn't see the fake news media and state governors going apeshit over that virus infection and case rate. The country didn't close down for the H1N1. What's different? Who's the president is what's different.

Source: [https://www.cdc.gov/flu/pandemic-resources/2009-h1n1-pandemic.html].

207,816 Dead from H1N1 (If We Treated H1N1 like COVID-19)

Imagine if, in 2009, the CDC changed the way they filled out death certificates as they have done for COVID-19. Then anyone who died with a positive test for H1N1 would be labeled an H1N1 death.

To end the H1N1 pandemic, the U.S. purchased 160 million doses of vaccine to circumvent the pandemic. The vaccine was rolled out too fast and subsequently caused health issues. It is reported that there were 12,469 U.S. deaths from the H1N1 swine flu.

Source: [http://www.nbcnews.com/id/32122776/ns/health-cold_and_flu/t/swine-flu-could-sicken-over-billion-years/].

Source: [https://www.globalresearch.ca/video-dr-anthony-fauci-on-the-2009-h1n1pandemic-the-2009-h1n1-vaccine-caused-brain-damage-in-children/5711540].

If we extrapolate that 12,469 is just 6% of the total death number, to make it similar to the same inflation factor used for COVID-19, then the reported death for H1N1 would be 207,816 deaths.

Wayback: How We Dealt with The Hong Kong Flu 1968-1969

In December of 1968, the Hong Kong flu is detected in the United States. This documented case initiated the flu pandemic that peaked the following year in 1969. This strain of flu would eventually kill 100,000 Americans. Most of the people who died from this flu were over 65 years old. This death number represents real deaths. Not like the fake inflated death numbers used for COVID-19.

The population of the United States was approximately 200 million. In comparison to today, with a population of 330 million people. If we extrapolate the Hong Kong flu's death rate using today's population, it is estimated, it would have killed 250,000 people. Again, this is a real death number, not inflated.

The United States government did not impose any lockdowns. There was no government intrusion into the lives of people. The media covered the pandemic without hysteria. People lived their lives in 1968-1969; when you look back, 1969 is remembered for Woodstock, not the Hong Kong flu. In today's world, Woodstock would have been shuttered.

1.6 Million Dead from Hong Kong Flu (If We Treated Hong Kong Flu Like COVID-19)

If we extrapolate that 100,000 Hong Kong flu is just 6% of the total death number, to make it similar to the same inflation factor used for COVID-19, then the reported deaths for the Hong Kong flu would be around 1.6 million deaths. And this is using the 200 million population numbers, not the current 330 million, which would increase the death rate.

How the United States dealt with the H1N1 and Hong Kong flu were proper responses. What happened today with the COVID-19 is political.

Chapter 3: The Politicized Pandemic

Bill Maher, the Democrat's Prophet

In June 2018, Bill Maher told his audience and followers, "One way you get rid of Trump is a crashing economy, so please bring on the recession. Sorry if that hurts people, but it's either root for a recession or lose your democracy."

Source: [https://pjmedia.com/news-and-politics/charlie-martin/2018/06/09/we-need-a-recession-to-save-us-from-trump-n58589].

The liberals were still hurting from three years of one failed impeachment scam after another.

Truth and the Country be Damned

As stated earlier, only the experts who supported the virus pandemic hysteria were trotted out and interviewed. Now I have the opportunity to list the institutions and doctors that were ignored or reported so minimally as to be virtually ignored because they didn't support fanning the flames of the COVID-19 hysteria.

Institutions Ignored	Scientists and Doctors Ignored
New England Journal of Medicine Stanford University	Dr. Michael Levitt – Nobel Prize winner in chemistry Dr. John Ioannidis – Epidemiologist, Stanford University Anders Tegnell – Sweden's top epidemiologist Dr. Simone Gold – America's Frontline Doctors Founder Dr. Jennifer Lighter – Epidemiologist, NYU Langone Health Dr. Alan Preston Senator Scott Jensen, MD Dr. Eran Bendavid Dr. Judy Mikovits – Censored on YouTube Dr. Annie Bukacek – Whistleblower CDC Death Certificates Dr. Dan Erickson – Censored on YouTube Dr. Artin Massihi – Censored on YouTube

The accurate threat assessment of COVID-19 was available from multiple sources before April 2020. Even so, as of July 2020, Democrat governors still had not ended the lockdown in their states.

Planning the Pandemic

Some may think the idea of the legacy fake news, social media, and Democrats tanking the U.S. economy is a bit of a far-fetched scenario. Consider the stakes. They could unseat President Trump, move the country into socialism, implement totalitarian control in Democrat-controlled states, and prepare the country for a great reset and new world order.

Farfetched? Who six months ago would have predicted that state governments would exert complete authoritarian control over the population to the point of closing businesses, schools, churches, and forcing people to stay home while suspending our constitutional rights?

The fact that "we the people" allowed this to occur illustrates the fake news fearmongering propaganda's brainwashing power! The constant inundation of COVID-19 misinformation convinced people to trade their freedoms for their promised illusion of safety. The fake news media and Democrats adopted the Nazi-style propaganda to explain their abusive actions taken against the population, *Fur Ihre Sicherheit* (translation *For Your Safety*).

President Trump's Travel Ban (January 2020)

President Trump issued a China travel ban on January 31, 2020, to prevent the spread of COVID-19 into the United States. The Democrats and fake news media attacked Trump's travel ban, calling the move overreacting and xenophobic. An action quickly adopted by other countries.

President Trump was months ahead of any Democrat leader in properly handling the COVID-19 threat to our country.

You'll never hear that from the fake news media. While Democrats were telling people not to worry and go about their business, President Trump took steps to limit the spread of the COVID-19 virus infection into the United States.

President Trump was also ahead of the CDC. Dr. Anthony Fauci, in January 2020, advised President Trump not to issue the travel ban.

Democrats Start Blaming President Trump for COVID-19 (February 2020)

Debating Democrats

During the Democratic primary debate on February 25, the candidates made false allegations that funding to the CDC and the National Institute of Health (NIH) was cut. In reality, their budget had increased.

AP Fact Check

The Associated Press published an article on February 26, "AP FACT CHECK: Democrats distort coronavirus readiness." The AP article pointed out that Michael Bloomberg and Joe Biden both falsely claimed that President Trump cut funding to the CDC.

Michael Bloomberg doubled down on his false allegations the next day by launching a thirty-second ad titled "Pandemic." This ad claimed the United States was underprepared for the coronavirus because of the cuts made by President Trump.

Source: [https://apnews.com/d36d6c4de29f4d04beda3db00cb46104].

Bernie Sanders Mocks the President

Bernie Sanders mocked President Trump during the primary debate, calling him a "self-described great genius" because Trump said the coronavirus outbreak would most likely dissipate in April. Meaning, as the warmer weather in April moved in, new cases of coronavirus flu would lower. A statement was concurrent with most influenza viruses.

Dr. Fauci, the director of the National Institute of Allergy and Infectious Diseases (NIAID), a man who has advised six presidents on domestic and global health issues, said this in an interview: "This history of respiratory viruses and other coronaviruses tend to diminish and almost disappear as you get into summer. It's just something that happens every year."

If I had Bernie's ear, I'd whisper, "Flu Season."

Councilwoman Candi CdeBaca

When a person on social media stated that if they were to come down with the coronavirus, they're "attending every MAGA rally, I can" to spread the infection to Trump supporters, and Democrat Denver Councilwoman Candi CdeBaca tweeted her support "#solidarity Yaaaas!!" Source: [https://t.co/PhgyQoWmPo]. This was tweeted by Councilwoman CdeBaca (@CandiCdeBacaD9) on February 28, 2020.

San Francisco

San Francisco's city has a homeless problem, as well as people defecating and urinating in the streets, rampant drug use, and more issues that stem from these. So, what decisive action does San Francisco take? The city officials declared a state of emergency for the coronavirus. Keep in mind, at this point, they didn't have a single confirmed case of coronavirus in their city.

New York Times - Trumpvirus

The *New York Times* decided to publish an op-ed piece, "Let's Call It Trumpvirus." They wanted to call the coronavirus the "Trumpvirus." Why? Did President Trump create the virus in his lab? No, that's what the Chinese scientists did. This shows the New York Times' bias toward President Trump since before his inauguration as president. Could you ever imagine the *New York Times* would publish an op-ed piece like this if it were about President Obama and the "swine flu" virus?

I get it. The liberal press (including the *New York Times*) and the Democrats hate President Trump. They hated him so much they were rooting for and promoting a pandemic to use it against him.

Laura Ingraham posted a Media Research Center (MRC) analysis of forty-four guest interviews on CNN. Out of the 136 questions that hosts asked about the epidemic, eighty-two (60 percent) asked guests to criticize the Trump administration. See the video here: [https://www.youtube.com/watch?v=-4bKdUx929s&feature=youtu.be].

Nancy Pelosi Encouraging People to Assemble and Shop (Feb. 24, 2020)

You won't hear the fake news show Democrat Congresswoman Nancy Pelosi on February 24, 2020, in Chinatown, urging people to assemble and shop.

Source: [https://www.foxnews.com/politics/trump-hits-pelosi-for-urging-crowds-to-assemble-in-chinatown-as-coronavirus-spread].

March 9, 2020 - Democrats Still Dancing in the Street

Until mid-March 2020, all the experts and most Democrat leaders told people not to worry about COVID-19. This included NIAID director Dr. Fauci, New York City Mayor Bill de Blasio, and others. As late as March 9, 2020, Dr. Fauci stated that attending campaign rallies and taking a cruise trip was okay.

Trump's Speech to the Nation (March 11, 2020)

President Trump addressed the nation. His speech had one purpose: to quell the irrational fears of the country regarding the COVID-19 coronavirus. Our nation's dangers are great, but they stem from the hysteria created by the ignorant rantings from the mainstream media press, not the coronavirus.

So, like a parent who has to alleviate a child's fears, the fake news press convinced about a boogeyman under their bed, President Trump spoke to the nation. He informed us that if there *is* a boogeyman under the bed, we're going to handle it. President Trump placed new travel restrictions from Europe. He reaffirmed our nation's strength, politically, financially, and morally. He reaffirmed our resiliency to handle this and any other crisis that comes up.

Practically, he calmed the frightened child and responded to the growing hysteria propagated by the fake mainstream media.

If I Had the Nation's Ear

If I could have addressed the nation, my statement would have been, "Yes, there's a threat, but it is a minor threat. Emphasize the word *minor*. If examined, the COVID-19 hysteria reporting doesn't stand up to scientific scrutiny. Stop believing the fake news hysteria."

President Trump Declares a National Emergency (March 13, 2020)

Declaring a national emergency was a green light for propagandizing worst-case speculation as fact, and suppressing, censoring, or deleting opposing information to that speculation.

Hidden Facts

If you theorize hindsight is twenty-twenty, and at that time, that was the best information available, you would be wrong. Remember the *NEJM* from February 28, 2020. Data gathered from over a thousand coronavirus cases between December 2019 and January 2020 showed that the coronavirus appeared to be *no worse than the seasonal flu* with a fatality rate (they expected to be) less than 1 percent. Even that low estimate from the *NEJM* turned out to be too high by a factor of three.

Source: [https://www.nejm.org/doi/full/10.1056/NEJMoa2002032?query=RP].

As early as March 17, 2020, the COVID-19 infection transmission rate from asymptomatic carriers had been estimated at a lowly 10 percent. Was this information correctly reported or publicized? No.

Source: [https://www.medicalnewstoday.com/articles/covid-19-study-estimates-rate-of-silent-transmission].

Social Media Censorship – The Arbitrators of Truth

Propagandizing the COVID-19 threat with misinformation wasn't enough. The fait accompli was censoring COVID-19 information that didn't meet or "violated" a social media community standard. What are the social media community standards? They are whatever social media platforms say they are. The social media "standards" are not enforced equally among users. Conservatives have long complained that their issues like "Pro-Life," "Pro Guns," "America First" are unfairly censored as being "hate speech."

Social media platforms actively "police" their platform. They are their arbitrators of truth. Like it or not, these platforms influence and inform millions of people. So, their censorship of conservative leaders, politicians, pundits, ideas, and posts has a chilling effect on the national consciousness. The social media platforms know this and leverage it to promote their agenda.

These platforms include YouTube, Facebook, Twitter, and Google. The censoring of information is so extensive, it can't be covered in a few paragraphs, so I devote Chapter 6 to social media censorship.

Why?

What could be the reason to promote a Scamdemic?

The Scamdemic is the tool used to force totalitarian lockdowns, strip citizens of their constitutional rights, and train the population into strict government obedience. It was also used against President Trump politically and forced massive insecure mail-in voting to accomplish massive fraud in the 2020 presidential election.

If you picked up this book, you already know the liberals on the left have lost their collective minds. The leftist legacy fake news media, hi-tech social media platforms, and the socialist Democrats are politically aligned and are activists against free speech, capitalism, conservatism, police, military, and promote their socialist "cancel culture" censorship.

This type of anti-American censorship was only seen in communist-controlled countries like China and Russia. Now social media platforms and legacy media openly censor anything that doesn't forward their agenda. They censor conservatives and conservative issues (like Christianity, pro-gun, and pro-life). They censor information that doesn't promote the China Virus as a pandemic and treatment options like hydroxychloroquine. They censor information that defies the socioeconomic lockdowns. They censor information that could hurt Democrat candidates' elections or cost them votes, like the Hunter Biden scandals. They censor evidence on the presidential election voter fraud.

Flipping the Country into Socialism – The Great Reset

Hasn't this Scamdemic pushed our country toward socialism and government totalitarianism? Americans are more dependent upon the government because of the scamdemic's socioeconomic shutdown? Millions of Americans are unquestioningly obedient to ridiculous lockdown regulations and will attack other Americans who don't follow.

How many Americans will remain dependent upon the government handouts because they and the businesses they work for will not recover and reopen after the lockdowns end?

Isn't this what the socialist democrats want, a totalitarian government with an obedient population? The process has taken a great leap forward. Beginning with media censorship, less capitalism, less constitutional freedoms, and greater control over businesses, industry, and production. What is the Great Reset? Reset into what, global socialism? Is that what Joe Biden's credo means to, "Build Back Better."

Sixty-four percent (64%) of Restaurants Permanently Closed

Already, sixty-four percent of restaurants will never reopen because of the forced shut-down as of September 2020. As lockdowns continue in December 2020 and into January 2021, we can expect the number of permanent business closures to increase.

Source: [https://www.forbes.com/sites/carlieporterfield/2020/09/04/a-staggering-64-of-new-york-restaurants-could-shut-for-good-by-2021-analysis-says].

How many other businesses, both small and large, will never reopen because of the forced lockdown?

President Donald Trump – The Haters

President Trump has many haters; socialists, fascist Democrats, leftist legacy media, and hi-tech social media platforms. To this, we can add the following.

Pro-Illegal Immigration – Trump curtailed illegal immigration, and haters include any businesses that exploited the cheap labor of ***illegal*** immigrants, as well as the politicians whom these businesses supported.

Silicon Valley – Trump limited the H1-B visa immigration, to the chagrin of Silicon Valley. High-tech companies like Google, Twitter, and Apple collaborate with China's CCP regime to be allowed entry into the Chinese marketplace. Twitter has no problem labeling and censoring

President Trump and his supporters. False information about COVID-19 from China's CCP, not so much.

Source: [https://spectator.us/twitter-china-pocket-jack-dorsey-marco-rubio/].

Mexico and Canada – Trump stopped Mexico and Canada from taking advantage of the U.S. Trump renegotiated the NAFTA trade agreement to the American worker's benefit with a fairer USMCA.

China – Donald Trump had warned the U.S. about China for decades before he became president. As president, Trump is stopping China from taking advantage of the U.S. by renegotiating our trade agreement with China to benefit the American worker.

On July 16, 2020, Attorney General William Barr gave a speech regarding the ongoing danger from the People's Republic of China. China is guilty of many illegal activities, such as currency manipulation, tariffs, quotas, state-led investments and acquisitions, theft, forced transfer of intellectual property, state subsidies, dumping, cyberattacks, industrial espionage. Eighty percent of all federal economic espionage prosecutions are to the benefit of the CCP. Sixty percent of trade secret theft is connected to China.

And let's not forget it was China who released the COVID-19 virus into the world and then lied to cover it up.

China Update:

Even more shocking is a leaked video made by a high-ranking college professor in China. He explained how they (the Chinese) had purchased influence from high-ranking officials in the United States and Wall Street. He complained that they (China) could NOT influence President Trump in disputes, but since Biden was elected, they expect more flexibility in the future. The speaker also inferred that they (CCP) helped finance the Biden foundation, to which his Chinese audience applauded.

Joe Biden started a foundation in 2017. In the first year, it raised 6.6 million dollars. Joe Biden suspended the operation of his Biden Foundation in April 2019 to focus on his Presidential Campaign.

The China video has been deleted off YouTube, no surprise there, but Tucker Carlson did a show segment on it and played the video for his audience. You can still view the piece and the Chinese video on the Fox News website here:

[https://video.foxnews.com/v/6214769762001#sp=show-clips].

Hollywood – China is an enormous market. To give you an idea, *Ironman* sold to the Asian market for $650 million. So Hollywood is very pro-China and anti-Trump. Hollywood studios go as far as to modify and censor its movies and characters to appease and follow directives from the Chinese Communist Party.

NBA – China is a vast billion-dollar market for the NBA. The NBA is pro-China and anti-Trump. A pro-Hong Kong tweet from an NBA general manager was quickly deleted as the Chinese Communist Party scolded the NBA. The threat of a lost franchise for the NBA in China forced the GM to delete his tweet and apologize. The NBA is not allowed to voice any opinion critical of the CCP, such as supporting a free Hong Kong.

Silicon Valley, Hollywood, and the NBA have sold out their integrity to China.

NATO – Trump embarrassed the member nations who had been taking advantage of the U.S. and asked them to pay their fair share.

WHO – The World Health Organization has misled people with Chinese misinformation relating to COVID-19 and has been caught and called out by President Trump. The World Health Organization lied for China and helped hide the facts regarding COVID-19. The World Health Organization's misinformation that the mortality rate of COVID-19 was a whopping 3.4 percent to 4.5 percent was the primer in creating a fake pandemic.

Fake News Legacy Media – Trump has been calling out the fake news media for their biased and inaccurate reporting of his administration. Despite everything positive Trump has accomplished for the American people and his pro-American stance, 90 percent of media coverage has negative. Trump's successes and accomplishments are not reported or reported minimally.

Social Media - Previously, one would have to live under a communist government to experience the level of censorship and brainwashing social media giants Facebook, Twitter, Google, and YouTube employs to further their "truth" and their "agenda." As noted for Hollywood and the NBA, access to the vast Chinese market is worth hundreds of millions of dollars per year. I'm wondering if these hi-tech companies are in bed and financially intertwined with the CCP? That could explain their un-American non-patriotic bias and censorship they employ against President Trump and the United States people.

Democrats – The socialists have been chanting to impeach Trump from before he officially took office. He disrupted the status quo on both sides of the aisle in Washington.

Who Loves President Donald Trump?

American workers and patriots.

While under constant siege by the fake news mainstream media, social media, deep state, DOJ, FBI, half of the Republicans, and all of the Democrats, President Trump revitalized the American economy. He brought unemployment to its lowest levels in decades, renegotiated America's bad trade deals, brought back manufacturing jobs to the American worker, ended U.S. involvement in the fraudulent climate-change Paris accord, and eased ridiculous and unnecessary regulations.

This coronavirus con, this Scamdemic, is yet another attempt to accomplish what the Russian hoax and the Mueller investigation could not: hurt President Trump's reelection by bringing the U.S. economy to a grinding halt.

I'm not worried about a billionaire who lost millions of dollars to become a public servant.

I am worried about those poor politicians who became multimillionaires being a public servant.

Chapter 4: The COVID-19 Scamdemic (Making It Real)

ICL Prediction – March 16, 2020: Ground Zero

The global lockdown began with the flawed Imperial College London (ICL) predictive coronavirus infection and fatality model.

Graph from flawed ICL model that initiated the global lockdown.

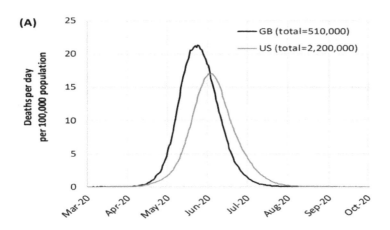

Neil M. Ferguson, Daniel Laydon, Gemma Nedjati-Gilani, et al. Impact of non-pharmaceutical interventions (NPIs) to reduce COVID-19 mortality and healthcare demand. Imperial College London (16-03-2020), [https://doi.org/10.25561/77482].

The world changed on March 16, 2020. What drove the United States and the rest of the world into this shelter-at-home, social-distancing, and economic lockdown? A flawed model from Professor Neil Ferguson, head of the MRC Centre for Global Infectious Disease Analysis at the ICL, who has a history of providing flawed disease models.

Source: [https://www.imperial.ac.uk/media/imperial-college/medicine/sph/ide/gida-fellowships/Imperial-College-COVID19-NPI-modelling-16-03-2020.pdf].

Neil Ferguson and the Imperial College London

Professor Ferguson released his non-peer-reviewed study with its secret algorithms in March. His model study predicted 500,000 deaths in the U.K. and 2.2 million deaths in the U.S.

Ferguson and ICL's Disastrous Track Record

Year	Ferguson's Prediction Failures	Results
2001	Convinced Tony Blair to kill 6 million heads of cattle to stop a foot-and-mouth disease. This move cost 10 billion pounds and needlessly killed millions of healthy animals. Source: [https://www.youtube.com/watch?v=rdI2YCh0FhA].	Only 178 people died.
2002	Predicted 50,000 would die from "Mad Cow Disease." If the disease transmitted to sheep, 150,000 more people would die.	
2005	Predicted up to 200 million people globally would die from bird flu H5N1.	Only 78 people died from the virus (2006).
2009	Predicted 65,000 people in the U.K. would die from swine flu.	Only 457 people died.

Ferguson has a disastrous track record of exaggerating the number of deaths from diseases. Anyone looking at his track record would become immediately suspicious of any study. See a summary in the table above.

Who, looking at the past predictions of Ferguson and the ICL, would not be suspicious of his current forecast?

Source: [https://www.telegraph.co.uk/news/2020/03/28/neil-ferguson-scientist-convinced-boris-johnson-uk-coronavirus-lockdown-criticised/].

Source: [https://www.dailymail.co.uk/news/article-8294439/ROSS-CLARK-Neil-Fergusons-lockdown-predictions-dodgy.html].

More Suspicious Clues Regarding the ICL Report

Neil Ferguson and the ICL team didn't release their secret coding algorithms for their program to make the predictions that 500,000 U.K. citizens and 2.2 million Americans would perish from COVID-19 without intervention. Releasing the algorithm is the proper etiquette and would have been allowed peer-review of the program's mathematics and results.

Instead, it took Neil Ferguson and the ICL team more than a month to release the program code for outside experts to examine.

Source: [https://www.telegraph.co.uk/news/2020/04/19/experts-largely-positive-computer-coding-thatled-coronavirus/].

There is an ongoing debate if the program released is the original program coding. This debate prompted repeated calls to the ICL to release its original program code.

Source: [https://www.aier.org/article/imperial-college-model-applied-to-sweden-yields-preposterous-results/].

University of Washington Confirms ICL

The University of Washington Institute for Health Metrics and Evaluation (IHME) in Seattle also predicted in March that our health care system would be overrun, seemly to confirm the ICL model.

Source: [https://www.medrxiv.org/content/10.1101/2020.03.27.20043752v1].

The only solution was to implement drastic lockdown measures.

First, They Duped President Trump, Then the Country

March 16, 2020. Dr. Anthony Fauci, director of NIAID and adviser to President Trump, received the ICL study. Dr. Fauci is a top-rated scientist. The ICL prediction model was not peered reviewed. The model's program and code were *not* released for examination. These two facts should have made Dr. Fauci skeptical of accepting this prediction.

The real scandal is Dr. Anthony Fauci accepting anything Neil Ferguson and the ICL predicted.

Sweden's chief epidemiologist Anders Tegnell, who received the same ICL report, discarded it.

The Okeydoke

Contrary to common sense, Dr. Fauci accepted the unverified, non-peer-reviewed ICL prediction from Neil Ferguson, who previously made awful predictions. Dr. Fauci, our country's top science adviser on disease, with his accomplice Dr. Deborah Birx, ran to President Trump and presented as fact a faulty prediction that stated 2.2 million Americans would die from COVID-19 unless drastic lockdown measures were taken.

Source: [https://www.imperial.ac.uk/media/imperial-college/medicine/sph/ide/gida-fellowships/Imperial-College-COVID19-NPI-modelling-16-03-2020.pdf].

Had Dr. Fauci conferred with Dr. John Ioannidis, an epidemiologist at Stanford University, or the New England Journal of Medicine researchers, we could have avoided this Scamdemic lockdown.

President Trump's intuition previous to Fauci's presentation was that this whole COVID-19 pandemic was overplayed. He was right, but the fake mainstream media mob was screaming to "follow the science."

Unfortunately, the "science," as it turns out, was Trump's own White House Coronavirus Task Force advisers Dr. Anthony Fauci and Dr. Deborah Birx.

Something Smells Rotten

Dr. Fauci, the director of NIAID, is one of our nation's top scientists. I struggle with the fact that neither Dr. Fauci nor anyone on his team never checked or knew about Neil Ferguson's previous faulty predictions. No due diligence on Ferguson's ICL report before presenting his prediction as fact to the president of the United States?

The lack of due diligence doesn't pass the smell test. Dr. Fauci, you advise the United States president on making a decision that affects over 300 million people and costing trillions of dollars. Didn't you double-check your information before advising him? I repeat, something smells rotten.

Consider if President Trump had been presented with the chart detailing Ferguson's previous prediction failures, shown above. Would he have taken the current prediction from Ferguson seriously?

As reported in the Gateway Pundit:

> **President Trump: "The big projection being that 2.2 million people would die if we did nothing. That was another decision we made—close it up. That was a big decision that we made. Two very smart people walked into my office and said, listen, these are your alternatives. And that was a projection of 1.5 to 2.2 million people would die if we didn't close it up. That's a lot of people."**

Those two "very smart" people were Dr. Anthony Fauci and Dr. Deborah Birx.

Source: [https://www.thegatewaypundit.com/2020/05/will-dr-fauci-dr-birx-serve-time-prison-destroying-us-economy-based-ridiculous-imperial-college-model-now-proven-complete-trash/].

More Real News Ignored

March 17, 2020

Dr. John Ioannidis, an epidemiologist at Stanford University, on March 17, 2020, one day after the Neil Ferguson, ICL (Imperial College London), announced 2.2 million Americans would die from coronavirus, correctly wrote: "The current coronavirus disease, Covid-19, has been called a once-in-a-century pandemic. But it may also be a once-in-a-century evidence fiasco." He warned us, "we are making decisions without enough data."

Source: [https://www.statnews.com/2020/03/17/a-fiasco-in-the-making-as-the-coronavirus-pandemic-takes-hold-we-are-making-decisions-without-reliable-data/].

The fake news media ignored him. We know today he was correct.

Additional scientific information released near the end of March 2020 also showed the COVID-19 threat was exaggerated, as reported by the *New England Journal of Medicine*, Stanford University, Dr. Anthony Fauci (adviser to President Trump). Even the Imperial College of London (ICL), whose prediction that 2.2 million American lives would be lost, revised its forecast downward dramatically from 2.2 million to 88,000. But this revision and backpedaling of the pivotal ICL projection, which caused the global lockdown, was not reported by the mainstream media fake news with the same veracity. Doing so would expose the fake news narrative.

Source: [https://thefederalist.com/2020/03/26/the-scientist-whose-doomsday-pandemic-model-predicted-armageddon-just-walked-back-the-apocalyptic-predictions/].

Source: [https://www.nejm.org/doi/pdf/10.1056/NEJMe2002387?articleTools=true].

Source: [https://www.nejm.org/doi/full/10.1056/NEJMoa2002032?query=RP].

March 25, 2020

Stanford stated that the fatality rate quoted in the ICL model was by order of great magnitudes exaggerated. "If it's true that the novel coronavirus would kill millions without shelter-in-place orders and quarantines, then the extraordinary measures being carried out in cities and states around the country are surely justified. **But there's little evidence to confirm that premise—and projections of the death toll could plausibly be orders of magnitude too high.**"

Source: [https://fsi.stanford.edu/news/coronavirus-deadly-they-say].

March 26, 2020
ICL Death Predictions Reduced by 96% (No Fake News Press)

On March 26, the dire predictions from Neil Ferguson of 500,000 U.K. deaths were reduced to 20,000 deaths. That's a 96 percent reduction in deaths predicted. While this reduction in deaths was noted in news reporting for the U.K., I haven't seen the reductions applied to the U.S. numbers. If we use the same percentage reduction, the ICL prediction lowers to 88,000 deaths in the U.S.

None of this information was reported by the fake news media and therefore did not make it into the public consciousness. Why? Because it did not fit the liberal mainstream media agenda. Nor did this reversal of the dire predictions from ICL's Neil Ferguson impact any state lockdown in the U.S.

Source: [https://www.washingtontimes.com/news/2020/mar/26/uk-epidemiologist-radically-lowers-his-predicted-c/].

Source: [https://dailycaller.com/2020/03/26/neil-ferguson-coronavirus-imperial-college-doomsday/].

The ICL Ferguson Hustle

Neil Ferguson and the ICL explained that the reduction in the projection deaths have to do with the "policies adapted," meaning the lockdown policies, quarantines, face masks, and social distancing are having their desired effect on reducing COVID-19 deaths, *but* he also modified his program code to use a lower case fatality rate (CFR).

Source: [https://reason.com/2020/03/27/no-british-epidemiologist-neil-ferguson-has-not-drastically-downgraded-his-worst-case-projection-of-covid-19-deaths/].

Not So Fast Mate: I'll Take Sweden for the Win

Remember the program the ICL released for examination? While the ICL released only predictions for the U.S. and the U.K., the program is in theory adaptable for any country. A team of researchers at Uppsala University used the ICL program to predict the COVID-19 model for Sweden. The team created an "unmitigated" response, which is the "do nothing" response. The ICL model predicted catastrophic results unless

Sweden followed emergency lockdown procedures adopted in the U.S., U.K., and the rest of Europe.

The ICL model predicted 40,000 deaths by May 1, 2020, ballooning to 96,000 Swedish deaths by June 30, 2020. The confidence interval of the ICL model was between 52,000 deaths and 183,000 deaths.

Sweden's government, fortunately, did not follow the ICL model predictions and recommendations to lockdown. Nor did Sweden's government bend its knee to the hysterical ranting of the fake news media.

Sweden stood tall and did *not* lock down their country. Businesses, restaurants, and stores remained open. Sweden asked its citizens to follow common sense and mild interventions—like, if you're sick, stay home, wash your hands, that kind of stuff. Sweden's death toll stood at 2,461 on April 29, 2020. Far below the dire 40,000 deaths predicted by the ICL model.

And for all the fake news reporting and hysteria about Sweden that followed their decision not to lock down, their death toll rates were lower than the United Kingdom, Italy, France, and other countries that did impose the draconian lockdowns on their citizens and businesses. Sweden pulled far ahead economically and intellectually.

The ICL model failed, big time! Don't expect to hear that in the fake news media.

Source: [https://www.aier.org/article/imperial-college-model-applied-to-sweden-yields-preposterous-results/].

If we extrapolate this response to the United States, it becomes apparent we've been hustled. Grab your old platform shoes and play some disco music and...do the hustle!

IHME Predicted Sweden Will Have 2,300 Deaths per Day

On May 3, 2020, the IHME predicted that unless Sweden followed the global trend to lock down its country with draconian measures, up to 2,300 Swedes would die daily within eleven days. It predicted a total of 75,000 deaths.

Sweden didn't lockdown, and the predicted deaths by the IHME never occurred.

Source: [https://www.herald.ng/fear-groupthink-drove-global-lockdowns/].

The Big Takeaway — Ignore the Truth Behind the Curtain

The fear for the fake news media is when people, or in this case a country, do not follow their panic-stricken lockdown orders and their dire predictions of death and destruction do not come to pass; it exposes them for the fake news that they are.

Like how that fake news reporter was exposed during Hurricane Florence.

That's what Sweden has done—exposed the fake news media, government agencies, and politicians. Our government officials have bamboozled you with their "safer lockdown" decisions by saying something to the effect of, "Well, we don't know what would have happened if we didn't implement these lockdowns, or how many millions of people may have died."

That's not true. We do know; Sweden showed us. Do the hustle!

Neil Ferguson Admits Sweden Achieved the Same Without Lockdown

Neil Ferguson admitted that Sweden achieved the same repression of the COVID-19 virus without the draconian lockdowns imposed in the U.K. and U.S.

Source: [https://www.dailymail.co.uk/news/article-8379769/Professor-Lockdown-Neil-Ferguson-admits-greatest-respect-Sweden.html].

Source: [https://www.telegraph.co.uk/news/2020/06/02/prof-lockdown-neil-ferguson-admits-sweden-used-science-uk-has/].

Do the hustle!

Fakes News – Sweden Has Not Done as Well as Other Norwegian Countries

Fake news is quick to point out that Sweden has not done as well regarding COVID-19 as other Nordic countries that did lockdown.

Real News - Sweden Has Done Better than the US, UK, France, and Italy

What fake news fails to point out is that Sweden has done better than the United States, England, France, and Italy who institute draconian lockdowns. What is that telling you about lockdowns and fake news?

Chapter 5: Fake News Agenda

The people will believe what the media tells them to believe. – George Orwell

With the president declaring a national emergency and the fraudulent ICL prediction reported as fact, the fake mainstream media news had the credibility it needed to propagandize the COVID-19 pandemic at warp speed.

Repeat A Lie Often Enough, It Becomes the Truth

The first law of propaganda: If you "repeat a lie often enough, it becomes the truth." This saying is often attributed to the Nazi Joseph Goebbels. The fake news mainstream media mentioned COVID-19 coronavirus over 2.1 billion times in March 2020. The fake news inundated the media with misinformation and reported from experts that agree with the virus hysteria to panic the population and allowed state governors to declare state emergencies.

Not a Black Swan Event, More Like a Perfect Storm

A black swan event is something that happens out of the ordinary—a rare, surprise occurrence. COVID-19 was not a black swan event. We get these viral pandemic occurrences once or twice a decade. The last pandemic was the H1N1, and the one before that was the Hong Kong Flu. So, the COVID-19 event was more of a perfect storm. A collaboration of liberal fake mainstream media, social media, and Democrat politicians to hype and weaponize an unknown flu strain against President Trump.

To make this point:

We've Been Here Before—2009 H1N1

In 2009 the U.S. had a flu pandemic. It began in April 2009, and by October 2009, there were at least 20,000 cases and more than a thousand deaths in the U.S. before then-President Obama reacted and called a national emergency.

Source:
[https://www.cnn.com/2009/HEALTH/10/24/h1n1.obama/index.html].

Could you imagine what the fake news media and socialist Democrats would say if President Trump waited until a thousand people died from COVID-19 before declaring a national emergency?

Dr. Fauci and the CDC under the Obama administration told the public that up to 40 percent of the American population might become infected with the H1N1 swine flu virus, resulting in 700,000 deaths over the next two years if a vaccine wasn't developed. The WHO declared up to two billion people worldwide could be infected.

The CDC reported over 60,000,000 Americans were infected with the H1N1 virus. That's more than 15X the number of people "infected" with COVID-19. But you didn't see the fake news media and state governors going apeshit over that virus infection and case rate. The country didn't close down for the H1N1. What's different? Who's the president is what's different.

207,816 Dead from H1N1 (If We Treated H1N1 like COVID-19)

Imagine if, in 2009, the CDC changed the way they filled out death certificates as they have done for COVID-19. Then anyone who died with a positive test for H1N1 would be labeled an H1N1 death.

To end the H1N1 pandemic, the U.S. purchased 160 million doses of vaccine to circumvent the pandemic. The vaccine was rolled out too fast and subsequently caused health issues. It is reported that there were 12,469 U.S. deaths from the H1N1 swine flu.

Source: [http://www.nbcnews.com/id/32122776/ns/health-cold_and_flu/t/swine-flu-could-sicken-over-billion-years/].

Source: [https://www.globalresearch.ca/video-dr-anthony-fauci-on-the-2009-h1n1pandemic-the-2009-h1n1-vaccine-caused-brain-damage-in-children/5711540].

If we extrapolate that 12,469 is just 6% of the total death number, to make it similar to the same inflation factor used for COVID-19, then the reported death for H1N1 would be 207,816 deaths.

Wayback: How We Dealt with the Hong Kong Flu 1968-1969

In December of 1968, the Hong Kong flu is detected in the United States. This documented case initiated the flu pandemic that peaked the following year in 1969. This strain of flu would eventually kill 100,000 Americans. Most of the people who died from this flu were over 65 years old. This death number represents real deaths. Not like the fake inflated death numbers used for COVID-19.

The population of the United States was approximately 200 million. In comparison to today, with a population of 330 million people. If we extrapolate the Hong Kong flu's death rate using today's population, it is estimated, it would have killed 250,000 people. Again, this is a real death number, not inflated.

The United States government did not impose any lockdowns. There was no government intrusion into the lives of people. The media covered the pandemic without hysteria. People lived their lives in 1968-1969; when you look back, 1969 is remembered for Woodstock, not the Hong Kong flu. In today's world, Woodstock would have been shuttered.

1.6 Million Dead from Hong Kong Flu? (If We Inflated Hong Kong Flu Deaths Like COVID-19)

If we extrapolate that 100,000 Hong Kong flu is just 6% of the total death number, to make it similar to the same inflation factor used for COVID-19, then the reported deaths for the Hong Kong flu would be 1.6 million deaths. And this is using the 200 million population numbers, not the current 330 million, which would double the death rate.

How the United States dealt with the H1N1 and Hong Kong flu were proper responses. What happened today with the COVID-19 is political.

This short 8-minute video shows how America dealt with the Hong Kong flu:

[https://www.youtube.com/watch?v=Ps5qIz06BzE&feature=emb_logo].

Now compare how the fake media has reported COVID-19 under President Trump.

Fox News

The fake news mainstream media's hatred of President Trump has been evident since before he took office. He has called them out repeatedly and appropriately named them "Fake News." So, promoting an unknown virus into hysteria to hurt President Trump explains the lack of investigative journalism in Neil Ferguson and the ICL report.

At the beginning of March, Fox News reported the "fake news" pandemic peddled by the mainstream media as exaggerations and a politicized tool being wielded against President Trump. The Fox News hosts included Trish Regan, Laura Ingraham, Sean Hannity, Jesse Watters, Tucker Carlson, and Judge Jeanine Pirro. Most of the hosts reported the mainstream media hype was to ruin the U.S. economy Trump had built up over the last three years.

Trish Regan, an influential Trump supporter, lovingly exposed the mainstream media and Democrats politicizing the COVID-19 virus with numerous news clips. She roasted the fake news and leftist Democrat politicians. Her show was so successful it was targeted by the liberal group Media Matters. I don't know if this group influenced Fox's management, but her show was put on hiatus on March 13, 2020, and later canceled on March 28, 2020.

In this time between March 13 and March 28, I observed a turnaround in reporting the COVID-19 virus on Fox News. Perhaps pushing Trish Regan's show off the air was management's warning to follow a more pro-hysteria COVID-19 reporting.

It's also possible that Fox was duped by Dr. Fauci and the flawed ICL prediction report. But that certainly doesn't explain Fox's lack of journalism into checking the ICL report and Neil Ferguson's history.

The following is a reference:

[https://www.lewrockwell.com/2020/05/no_author/the-dubious-covid-models-the-tests-and-now-the-consequences/].

Fake News Media in the Tank for the COVID-19 Pandemic

It's been months since Neil Ferguson, and the ICL released their COVID-19 prediction that shut down the global economy. In all this time, has the fake legacy media performed any due diligence on Neil Ferguson or the ICL projection? Not one phony legacy media outlet has published all the failed infection project from the past. You should be asking yourself why.

Source: [https://www.telegraph.co.uk/news/2020/03/28/neil-ferguson-scientist-convinced-boris-johnson-uk-coronavirus-lockdown-criticised/].

Source: [https://www.dailymail.co.uk/news/article-8294439/ROSS-CLARK-Neil-Fergusons-lockdown-predictions-dodgy.html].

Believe It, or Be Mocked

If you do not follow the narrative or contradict the report, then the mainstream media news uses Saul Alinsky's playbook *Rules for Radicals*. The most common tactic is to be mocked as a "denier." Labeled as a health risk, selfishly putting the lives of believers at risk. This label has caused many confrontations and fights and is used by social media platforms as justification to restrict and delete accounts.

The fake news's legacy media methodology is to shut down any dissenting information that questions their false narrative. The phony news labels such people as nonsensible "deniers" who blatantly disregard "proven" scientific facts that can therefore be dismissed. Being dismissed negates the legacy media's job to examine any conflicting points or answer any question.

Here are the few truth-tellers the fake news ignored or mocked:

- *New England Journal of Medicine*
- Stanford University
- Sweden
- Japan
- Taiwan

Social Media Censorship to the Rescue

Social media platforms censor dissenting information, labeling it "dangerous" and violating the platform's community standard. This outright censorship of dissenting information on the COVID-19 virus and the scamdemic prevails on YouTube, Twitter, and Facebook.

Similar tactics were employed to censor Joe Biden's family's financial dealings with other countries while Joe Biden was vice-president. They also censored any news regarding information found on Joe Biden's son Hunter Biden's laptop.

And again, any information regarding the fraud taking place in the 2020 election was censored, mocked, or labeled "disputed" by the legacy and social media. Supplemental information has been added to this book on the 2020 election.

Google uses the search engine manipulation effect (SEME) to achieve much of the same. There is too much information to cover this topic here, so I devoted Chapter 6 to high-tech censorship.

Chapter 6: Social Media Censorship

The left-leaning social media platforms silence opposing voices. The main three discussed here are Google, YouTube, and Facebook.

First, Google

Google's threat extends well beyond this fake pandemic; Google is a threat to democracy.

Google and the Google logo are registered trademarks of Google LLC, used with permission.

Google can censor information and propagandize information to align with its agenda without anyone knowing they have been manipulated.

Google Search Engine Bias

Google is biased. Books can be written documenting Google bias. I will look at only the two I feel have the most significant impact on our democracy. I am not hyperbolic that Google is a threat to democracy.

Google's Playbook: "The Good Censor"

The Good Censor is an eighty-five-page playbook created by Google that was leaked to Breitbart News in 2018. The playbook details how the idea of free speech on the internet is, in Google's viewpoint, a utopian ideal. Google's view is that this utopian ideal cannot be maintained on the internet partly because of "bad behavior" by the populace, which included electing Donald Trump, president of the United States. You can read Google's full eighty-five-page "The Good Censor" briefing for yourself on Breitbart.com.

Source: [https://www.breitbart.com/tech/2018/10/09/the-good-censor-leaked-google-briefing-admits-abandonment-of-free-speech-for-safety-and-civility/].

Google Goes to War Against President Trump

After Trump was elected president, a one-hour video was leaked from Google, where Google's top executives complained that Trump's election was a disaster and that they (Google) were never going to let this happen again.

You can view the leaked video here: [https://www.breitbart.com/tech/2018/09/12/leaked-video-google-leaderships-dismayed-reaction-to-trump-election/].

2016 Presidential Election – Voter Manipulation

Dr. Robert Epstein, a lifelong Democrat and Hillary Clinton supporter, monitored Google's search engine results. He used a group of ninety-five people located in twenty-four states for his study. He analyzed 13,000 searches and 98,000 web pages. He found, and I quote, "found very dramatic bias in Google's search results...favoring Hillary Clinton—whom I support strongly."

Dr. Epstein earned his Ph.D. in psychology at Harvard University in 1981. He was the editor-in-chief of the magazine *Psychology Today*. Currently, a senior research psychologist at the American Institute for Behavioral Research & Technology. He has been a research psychologist for forty years and published extensively on artificial intelligence and Google.

Dr. Epstein looked at the leaked Google video and examined what Google whistleblowers and employees who had quit Google have said. They told the same story. Google plans to use every technique at its disposal to shift votes away from President Trump and to his opponent in the 2020 election.

He testified before Congress to explain the Google bias he uncovered in the 2016 election. He prefaced his testimony by saying that while a Democrat and Hillary Clinton supporter, "I value my country and democracy more than I value any party or candidate. That is why I am speaking out today." He testified that Google is a serious threat to democracy. He determined that Google manipulated and shifted a minimum of 2.6 million undecided voters to vote for Hillary Clinton through his analysis. None of these 2.6 million undecided voters were aware that they were manipulated to vote for Hillary Clinton.

And by the way, those 2.6 million votes are a minimum number; the actual number of swayed votes may be relatively more.

How can Google do this? It turns out to be pretty straightforward if you're Google. The answer is the ranking of the search engine results. People believe Google is neutral and fair and will weigh the top page results more important than the bottom page. I mean, that's the way ranking is supposed to work. And that's what Google manipulates. In the case of the 2016 presidential election, it autocompleted, erased, or decreased the search volume ranking of any detrimental information about Hillary Clinton, such as her email scandal or Benghazi, while promoting any positive news for her. For the Trump campaign, Google oppositely manipulated its autocomplete results; questionable information regarding

Trump was promoted, while Trump's positive information was either erased or demoted in its search volume ranking. These driven search engine results subliminally shifted people's perception of the candidates to Hillary's favor. These manipulations leave no trail for authorities to uncover at a later date.

We can prove this Google manipulation because Dr. Epstein recorded all the search engine results for his study, so he has hard-copy proof.

Better than this, later, you can use the search engine manipulation effect (SEME) to prove Google bias yourself, using Google. No experience necessary.

SEME: Search Engine Manipulation Effect

After the 2016 presidential election, Google went to war. On March 3, 2020, Glenn Beck interviewed Dr. Epstein, where he stated that Google represents the biggest threat to our democracy. I agree. Dr. Epstein coined the term SEME for *search engine manipulation effect*, one of Google's psychological tools for influencing people without them being aware of the manipulation.

The SEME is not confined to manipulating millions of votes in the presidential elections; no, aside from its potential to overthrow democracy, it is wielding its influence in everything Google wants to influence. As it turns out, that's a lot.

From my preliminary work, Google is influencing the results for vaccinations and autism, information on COVID-19, and vitamin supplements. This, as they say, is the tip of the iceberg. From others, I am hearing they are demoting people in the natural health industry. Google is expanding its influence well beyond censoring conservatives.

Prove It for Yourself

I will show you a few simple techniques that you can use to prove to yourself that Google is using its search engine results to influence people the way Google wants them affected. Ready? Let's go.

Google's autocompleting is supposed to work when you type a term in Google search; you see Google offering predictions to autocomplete what you are typing. These "predictions," according to Google, are based on search volume and *not* suggestions. Predictions, not suggestions.

Just so no one thinks I'm putting words into Google's operating procedure mouth, below is a copy of how their predictive autocomplete is "supposed" to work.

Notice the title, "Predictions, not suggestions." The highlighted text states, "We look at the real searches that happen on Google and show the common and trending ones relevant to the characters that are entered and also related to your location and previous searches."

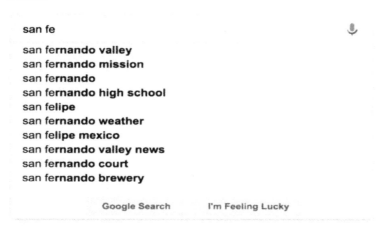

Predictions, not suggestions

You'll notice we call these autocomplete 'predictions' rather than 'suggestions,' and there's a good reason for that. Autocomplete is designed to help people complete a search they were intending to do, not to suggest new types of searches to be performed. These are our best predictions of the query you were likely to continue entering. How do we determine these predictions? We look at the real searches that happen on Google and show common and trending ones relevant to the characters that are entered and also related to your location and previous searches.

The predictions change in response to new characters being entered into the search box. For example, going from "san f" to "san fe" causes the San Francisco-related predictions shown above to disappear, with those relating to San Fernando then appearing at the top of the list:

san fe 🎤

san **fernando valley**
san **fernando mission**
san **fernando**
san **fernando high school**
san **felipe**
san **fernando weather**
san **felipe mexico**
san **fernando valley news**
san **fernando court**
san **fernando brewery**

Google Search   I'm Feeling Lucky

That makes sense. It becomes clear from the additional letter that someone isn't doing a search that would relate to San Francisco, so the predictions change to something more relevant.

Google and the Google logo are registered trademarks of Google LLC, used with permission.

Source: [https://www.blog.google/products/search/how-google-autocomplete-works-search/].

First Proof

To find out search volumes, we can use Google's tool "Google Trends."

The first trend I examine below is, "do vaccines cause autism."

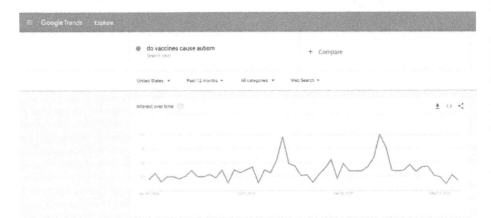

Google and the Google logo are registered trademarks of Google LLC, used with permission.

That graph represents the search volume of the term "do vaccines cause autism."

With this information, let's do a Google search and see what happens.

Google and the Google logo are registered trademarks of Google LLC, used with permission.

When we type the term "do vaccines cause a..." we can see how the autocomplete generates suggestions, supposedly based on search volume.

Okay, then the most search volume term is "do vaccines cause active or passive immunity." Let us plug that term into Google Trends to check its search volume.

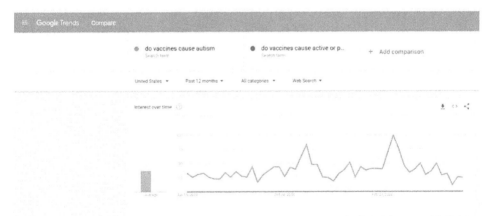

Google and the Google logo are registered trademarks of Google LLC, used with permission.

The search volume for "do vaccines cause active or passive immunity" is the flat red line in the chart above. Its search volume is zero. Yet Google's autocompleting is saying its search volume is higher than "do vaccines cause autism."

Let go further. If we continue typing in "do vaccines cause autism" in Google search, the Google artificial intelligence blocks it out of autocomplete entirely as if the term doesn't exist.

Google and the Google logo are registered trademarks of Google LLC, used with permission.

Google's parent company, Alphabet, has two pharmaceutical companies, Calico and Verily Life Sciences.

Second Proof

I can provide proof all day, but I'll do one more regarding COVID-19. Many people who researched the COVID-19 threat, as I did, realized the danger of the disease, not the disease, was mostly a hoax. So, our second Google search is "is COVID-19 a scam."

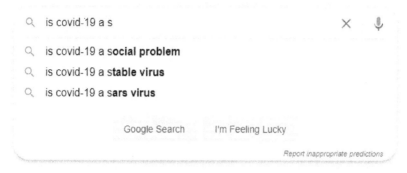

Google and the Google logo are registered trademarks of Google LLC, used with permission.

As I type the phrase into Google search, this is what happens. Google's autocompleting is suggesting that "is COVID-19 a social problem" is the most searched phrase.

Google and the Google logo are registered trademarks of Google LLC, used with permission.

The blue line in Google Trends shows the search for "is COVID-19 a scam," and the flat red line is the search for "is COVID-19 a social problem."

Again, we prove that Google is *not* using search volume to help people find the most relevant data when searching. They are suggesting what they want you to see based on Google's agenda.

And if we continue to type in "is COVID-19 a scam," again Google's AI blocks the phrase from showing relevant content; see below.

Google and the Google logo are registered trademarks of Google LLC, used with permission.

Look back at how Google states their autocomplete works: "Predictions, not suggestions."

In the body of their text, it further states: "We look at the real searches that happen on Google and show the common and trending ones relevant to the characters that are entered and also related to your location and previous searches."

2020 Election Time

Google began censoring conservative websites like Breitbart.com and Dailycaller.com by cutting their appearance in search results. **Google has reduced Breitbart search results by 99.7 percent.** This action will influence the 2020 presidential election in favor of the Democrat candidate. Any voter using Google on the internet for news and information will no longer be shown conservative opinions and news stories because Google is darkening conservative sites like Breitbart.

As we start to roll into the 2020 election cycle, the social media giants are bad actors behaving like the fake news media. They filter out opposing news and opinions that contradict their agenda—darkening conservative websites not to be searchable and viewed via their platforms. Actions they are permitted to take under the guise of "speech and information" that violate their arbitrary platform guidelines. These are no longer neutral platforms; these are manipulative propaganda activists.

Source: [https://www.breitbart.com/clips/2020/07/29/marlow-google-has-diminished-breitbart-search-results-99-7-big-tech-will-do-anything-in-their-power-to-get-biden-elected/].

It's Only a Matter of Time

It's only a matter of time before Google has its programmers modify its Google Trends output to sync with its autocompletion. At that point, its manipulation will be thoroughly hidden and undetectable. I hope experts like Dr. Epstein will still have techniques to check for Google's manipulations.

Yahoo

It appears Yahoo isn't as biased as Google. At least "is COVID-19 a scam" came up ranked number four, instead of not at all.

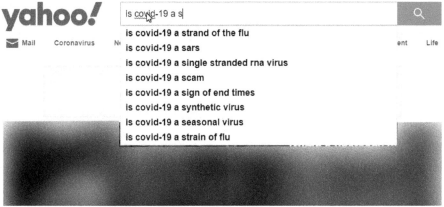

Courtesy of Yahoo.com and Verizon Media

Why Google?

Why would Google be interested in manipulating data on COVID-19 and vaccines? I know that Google's parent company, Alphabet Inc., also owns Verily, its life science division. Verily partnered with GlaxoSmithKline, the sixth-largest multinational pharmaceutical firm. And GlaxoSmithKline has partnered with Sanofi to develop a COVID-19 vaccine.

Google in the 2020 Presidential Election

Recently Dr. Robert Epstein claimed that Google would shift 10 percent of the vote away from President Trump. If Google is capable of turning this many votes, democracy is dead.

Source: [https://www.breitbart.com/tech/2020/07/10/dr-robert-epstein-google-will-shift-10-of-voters-to-make-trump-a-blip-in-history/].

YouTube Censorship

Google owns YouTube, so it's not surprising to see YouTube censoring information.

YouTube Deletes Any Video Contradicting WHO

YouTube is censoring any video contradicting the World Health Organization's policy. Why? Let's look back at the wrong information WHO gave to the world.

On March 3, 2020, WHO stated the fatality rate of COVID-19 is 3.4 percent to 4.5 percent, and only 1 percent of reported COVID-19 cases do not have symptoms.

Source: [https://www.who.int/dg/speeches/detail/who-director-general-s-opening-remarks-at-the-media-briefing-on-covid-19---3-march-2020].

This terrible and faulty information contributed to the unnecessary global lockdown that occurred. The actual fatality rate for COVID-19 is 0.3 percent, less than one-tenth of the fatality rate quoted by WHO. Further, 33 percent to 45 percent of COVID-19 cases are asymptomatic, up to forty-five times more people than initially quoted by WHO.

Had this factual information been provided, the United States would have never locked down. WHO's name ought to be changed to the World Hysteria Organization.

President Trump said WHO had a "role in severely mismanaging and covering up the spread of coronavirus." Further, "Had the WHO done its job to get medical experts into China to assess the situation on the ground objectively and to call out China's lack of transparency, the outbreak could have been contained at its source with very little death."

YouTube Deletes Doctors

YouTube is also deleting videos from doctors who disagree with any tyrannical state governors' unconstitutional and draconian lockdown measures.

Source: [https://www.breitbart.com/tech/2020/04/28/youtube-censors-video-of-california-doctors-calling-for-reopening-of-country/].

YouTube censors PragerU:
[https://www.prageru.com/petition/youtube/].

YouTube censors several videos by Dr. Judy Mikovits:
[https://youtubecensorship.com/2020-05-16-dr-judy-mikovits-interviewed-coronavirus-pandemic-fauci-nih-corruption.html].

YouTube censors critics of the Chinese Communist Party:
[https://www.theblaze.com/news/youtube-auto-censoring-criticism-chinese-communist-party].

YouTube Deleting All evidence of Election Fraud in 2020 Presidential Election.

Source:
[https://www.americanthinker.com/blog/2020/12/googleyoutube_is_erasing_all_evidence_of_election_fraud.html].

Facebook Censorship

Facebook is blocking COVID-19 information from any source its biased fact-checkers deem as incorrect information or "misinformation." They have blocked posts from many legitimate news sources like the *New York Post*, *Dallas Morning News*, *USA Today*, *The Independent*, etc.

Source: [https://www.foxnews.com/opinion/facebook-doesnt-really-believe-in-free-speech-what-they-believe-in-and-actively-practice-is-censorship].

Many substantiated claims claim that Facebook targets conservatives and uses liberal arbitrators to determine what is, or isn't, hate speech.

If you are pro-Trump, pro-gun, or pro-life, your posts are held to a different "hate speech" standard.

Source: [https://nypost.com/2020/04/17/facebook-fact-checkers-foul-again-after-censoring-post-story/].

According to a Fox News report, Facebook works with left-wing groups on "content moderation," elections, and creating a "civil rights accountability infrastructure."

Source: [https://www.forbes.com/sites/johnkoetsier/2020/03/17/facebook-deleting-coronavirus-posts-leading-to-charges-of-censorship/#3fb216a95962].

Facebook Bans Anti-Quarantine Events

Facebook deleted events organized by shelter-at-home protestors in New Jersey, Nebraska, California, and other places across the country.

Source: [https://nypost.com/2020/04/20/facebook-bans-anti-quarantine-event-protest-posts-in-mandatory-lockdown-states/].

Facebook Censors Alternative Social Distancing Information

During an interview with ABC News, Facebook founder and CEO Mark Zuckerberg stated alternative information regarding social distancing will be viewed as "harmful misinformation" and taken down. People using Facebook to this end were censored.

Facebook Censors Information on Hydroxychloroquine

Facebook removed videos and posts from Simone Gold and America's Frontline Doctors. See Chapter 12: Treating Covid-19 – Hydroxychloroquine for more information.

Source: [https://www.breitbart.com/tech/2020/07/28/dr-simone-gold-squarespace-shuts-down-americas-frontline-doctors-website/].

Amazon.com Censorship

Amazon is not a tech company. President Trump's chief complaint about Amazon is that the U.S. Postal Service doesn't charge enough for shipping Amazon's packages. The second complaint is that despite substantial corporate profits, Amazon pays little to no taxes. To this end, Jeff Bezos, the founder of Amazon, also owns the *Washington Post*, which attacks President Trump, his administration, and policies.

Amazon made it into this section, not for any of those reasons stated above. That's just background information. Amazon made it into this section for activating censoring the publication of COVID-19 books on its Kindle platform. Amazon is a publisher and has every right to decide what to allow to be published.

Amazon censored Alex Berenson's e-book *Unreported Truths about Covid-19*. When he informed his Twitter followers, one of his followers is Elon Musk, who wrote a few tweets that caused Amazon to unblocked Berenson's book.

Don't Be Complacent

Democracy and freedom are being threatened at every level by Google, YouTube, Facebook, and Twitter. There are alternative social media platforms opening that is not censored and politically biased.

MeWe

Mewe is a politically unbiased Facebook replacement

Go to: [https://mewe.com].

Join conservatives at: [https://mewe.com/join/unitedconservativesforabetteramerica].

Parler

Parler is a politically unbiased Twitter-like application.

Go to: [https://parler.com/auth/access].

LBRY

A politically unbiased replacement for YouTube is LBRY

Go to: [https://lbry.com/].

RUMBLE

Another politically unbiased replacement for YouTube is RUMBLE

Go to: [https://rumble.com/].

DuckDuckGo

An alternate search engine for Google is DuckDuckGo

DuckDuckGo doesn't collect personal information on your searches and is mainly used for privacy issues. It is not confirmed to be politically unbiased.

[https://duckduckgo.com/].

More are coming.

Poland Halts Big-Tech Censorship

Poland halted big-tech censorship by enacting an "online freedom of speech" law that allows the tech company to be sued for censoring free speech online. If a tech company illegally censors a post, the law allows that tech company to be sued for a maximum statutory damage of approximately 2.2 million dollars.

Source: [https://polandin.com/51388314/justice-minister-announces-online-freedom-of-speech-bill].

As every conservative individual, newsgroup, and website will attest, we need a similar law here in the United States.

Chapter 7: Lockdowns – Welcome to COVID-19*84*

LOCKDOWN
Covid-19 / Coronavirus

Despite the scientifically-backed evidence and information available to state governments at the end of March 2020, the states continued their massive socioeconomic shutdown based on unsubstantiated claims and model predictions!

All the pieces were in play. The legacy fake news media only reported it's pandemic agenda friendly information. At the same time, social media censored or labeled any conflicting information. The Democrats supported the fake news and used the fear panicked to seize emergency powers to implement totalitarian control over the states, promising safety.

States imposed lockdowns without consideration for the collateral damage these lockdowns would cause.

U.S. Annual Death By Disease

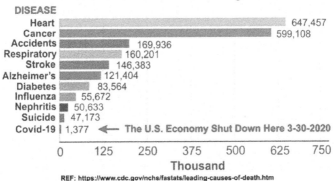

REF: https://www.cdc.gov/nchs/fastats/leading-causes-of-death.htm

We Never Closed Our Country Down for the Flu Before

We don't close our country down every year because of the flu. COVID-19 is just another type of flu. It is a virulent flu without a vaccine, so it may take a few more lives than influenza, but it is *not* the virus apocalypse predicted. And at this point, with all the inflated deaths being reported for COVID-19, I can't be sure if COVID-19 deaths have exceeded influenza deaths.

OBEY: Shelter at Home (You're Under House Arrest)

State governors across the U.S. invoked emergency powers and placed approximately 90 percent of their residents under quarantine and house arrest. To keep people home, under the pretense of slowing the spread of COVID-19, state governments have closed restaurants, movies, and shops, schools, churches, parks, and beaches.

Source: [https://www.cbsnews.com/video/90-of-americans-are-under-stay-at-home-orders/].

Any businesses the governor deemed nonessential closed. I don't understand why Governor Cuomo considered liquor stores and abortion clinics essential businesses in New York, but not dentists.

Anyone caught not following the state and city government guidelines would be fined $1,000 and brought to jail. Across the nation, parents were arrested and fined for visiting a park with their child. One man was fined $1,000 for surfing. Other people sitting in cars watching a sunset were fined $1,000.

Source: [https://www.latimes.com/california/story/2020-03-29/surfer-fined-1-000-for-ignoring-coronavirus-closure-in-manhattan-beach].

In August 2020, Los Angeles Mayor Eric Garcetti told city residents anyone breaking social distancing policies can expect to have their electrical power cut and water turned off. Just another Democrat's fascist policy.

If being placed under house arrest wasn't bad enough, the most egregious offense is suspending our constitutional rights. Residents lost their rights to assemble, protest the government, attend church and funerals, or visit loved ones in nursing homes.

Doctors and hospitals were forced to cancel elective surgeries, cancel diagnostic screenings, including cancer screening, blood tests, and therapies to prepare for a pandemic. A pandemic that never occurred.

OBEY: Mandatory Face Masks

The next sham perpetrated on the public was mandatory face masks for healthy people. I'm not telling anyone to wear or not to wear a face mask. I am presenting the data and information the fake news media will not.

Why Face Masks Fail: The Science of Particle Size

Face masks are worn to filter out harmful bacteria and viruses from entering your lungs.

The N95 masks are capable of filtering out 95 percent of particle matter larger than 0.3 microns. COVID-19 particle size is about 0.1 micron. Even though the N95 mask is not designed for a particle size of 0.1 microns, it is "believed" to be sufficient to filter out the COVID-19 virus. However, the N95 mask doesn't protect the eyes, which is another inroad for the virus to enter your body.

To provide some relative sizes, white blood cells are 25 microns, red blood cells 8 microns, and bacteria are ranging from 1 to 20 microns.

Surgical masks are useful to block particle matter at 5 microns or larger. So even the high-quality surgical masks are not effective at stopping COVID-19 virus particles.

This brings us to examine those cheap paper "dust" masks or homemade cloth masks. Wow, to say that they are not as effective as surgical masks is an understatement. As Senator Scott Jensen, MD, said, wearing face masks for protection against the COVID-19 virus is "looney tunes." Source: Senator Scott Jensen, MD, Republican, Minnesota.

Before I present the clinical studies showing that face masks are ineffective, let's first look where face masks are useful.

Health Care Workers Need Face Masks

If you're a health care worker treating patients sick with COVID-19 or the flu, an N95 face mask is mandatory. An N95 face mask can reduce the COVID-19 virus in the particulate matter being aspirated into the air from coughing or sneezing. But only if you are wearing an N95 mask—a standard surgical mask isn't much protection from the COVID-19 virus.

An N95 face mask is also necessary for anyone taking care of a COVID-19 symptomatic sick person at home. If you are sick, you should wear an N95 face mask, which will help prevent the disease's spread to others. These are legitimate reasons for wearing a face mask.

If you aren't dealing with infected, symptomatic people with COVID-19, washing your hands often offers a better precaution than a face mask.

Face Mask Sham – The Real Deal

While state governors issued new laws forcing healthy people to wear face masks to enter stores and other public facilities, scientific clinical studies don't support these laws.

Study after study shows the **lack of effectiveness** in wearing face masks to stop the spread of viral disease in a community. Face masks *do not* significantly prevent the spread of respiratory viruses. The *New England Journal of Medicine* published an article in April 2020 stating that numerous previous clinical studies and trials call out this practice as nonsense.

Source: [https://www.cambridge.org/core/journals/epidemiology-and-infection/article/face-masks-to-prevent-transmission-of-influenza-virus-a-systematic-%20review/64D368496EBDE0AFCC6639CCC9D8BC05].

Source: [https://onlinelibrary.wiley.com/doi/epdf/10.1111/j.1750-2659.2011.00307.x].

New England Journal of Medicine Dismisses Face Masks

"We know that wearing a mask outside health care facilities offers little if any, protection from infection. Public health authorities define a significant exposure to Covid-19 as face-to-face contact within 6 feet with a patient with symptomatic Covid-19 sustained for at least a few minutes (and some say more than 10 minutes or even 30 minutes). The chance of catching Covid-19 from a passing interaction in a public space is therefore

minimal. In many cases, the desire for widespread masking is a reflexive reaction to anxiety over the pandemic."

Source: [https://www.nejm.org/doi/full/10.1056/NEJMp2006372].

Face Mask – Randomized Controlled Trial

Let's put the science of size to the side and look at previous face mask studies.

Eleven randomized controlled trials and ten observational studies could *not* statistically show that wearing face masks in a community setting reduced viral respiratory infections. The results of all these studies were equivocal.

Source: [https://www.qeios.com/read/1SC5L4].

What Face Masks Are You Wearing?

There are face masks, and there are face masks. Members of the public are not wearing respirators, surgical masks, or N95 masks. Most of the inexpensive face masks worn by the public are dust masks that "may" protect against bacteria, but not the COVID-19 virus. Unfortunately, wearing even an ineffectual face mask may lull the wearer into thinking they are better protected than they are. This false confidence may cause the wearer to become lax in other sanitary measures like hand cleaning, and therefore they may be more likely to catch an infection.

Homemade Cloth Mask May Increase Risk Of Infection

If you think those homemade cloth masks are any better, think again. Aside from the science of size above, according to a Pubmed.gov study, cloth masks will increase your likelihood of infection. "Moisture retention, reuse of cloth masks, and poor filtration may result in an increased risk of infection."

Source: [https://pubmed.ncbi.nlm.nih.gov/25903751/].

Another study of 1,600 healthcare works found that "Penetration of cloth masks by particles was almost 97% and medical masks 44%." They reached the following conclusion. "This study is the first RCT of cloth masks, and the results caution against the use of cloth masks."

Source: [https://bmjopen.bmj.com/content/5/4/e006577].

Why You Shouldn't Wear a Face Mask

Aside from face masks being ineffectual in protecting from viral infections, there are legitimate and legal reasons not to wear face masks.

1. Face masks may reduce your blood oxygen level. Depending upon your health, this could be serious. This is most likely for people who have or are predisposed to breathing issues, like a smoker, obese, or have COPD or asthma. You would need a pulse oximeter to check your blood oxygen level and determine the impact a face mask has upon it. But if you have asthma or any breathing issue, ask to be exempt. Researchers claim that the N95 face mask can reduce oxygen intake by 5 percent to 20 percent. That is significant.

2. Anyone exercising should not wear a face mask. It will lower your blood oxygen levels and increase your blood carbon dioxide levels while exercising.

   Sweating while exercising will get the face mask damp, making it subsequentially harder to breathe through the mask, exacerbating lower blood oxygen levels and increased carbon dioxide levels. Having a wet mask will also promote the growth of bacteria and microorganisms, affecting your health.

   Source: [https://www.newsmax.com/health/health-news/face-mask-oxygen/2020/05/27/id/969226/].

Source: [https://technocracy.news/blaylock-face-masks-pose-serious-risks-to-the-healthy/].

Source: [http://scielo.isciii.es/pdf/neuro/v19n2/3.pdf].

Face Mask Flip-Flops

March 2, 2020 – U.S. Surgeon General Jerome Adams stated that wearing masks is not a preventive to spreading the disease.

Source: [https://video.foxnews.com/v/6137596907001#sp=show-clips].

April 1, 2020 – The *New England Journal of Medicine* wrote, "We know that wearing a mask outside health care facilities offers little if any, protection from infection. Public health authorities define a significant exposure to Covid-19 as face-to-face contact within 6 feet with a patient with symptomatic Covid-19 sustained for at least a few minutes (and some say more than 10 minutes or even 30 minutes). The chance of catching Covid-19 from a passing interaction in a public space is therefore minimal. In many cases, the desire for widespread masking is a reflexive reaction to anxiety over the pandemic."

Source: [https://www.nejm.org/doi/full/10.1056/NEJMp2006372].

April 5, 2020 – Dr. Fauci said in his statement that "The major reason to wear a face mask is to protect you from infecting you."

April 6, 2020 – U.S. Surgeon General Jerome Adams reversed his March 2, 2020 position.

May 27, 2020 – Dr. Fauci reversed himself, saying he wears a face mask in public, "because I believe it is effective. ... I do it when I am in public for the reason that I want to protect myself and protect others, and also because I want to make it be a symbol for people to see that that's the kind of thing you should be doing."

December 2020 – Dr. Fauci admits to lying to the public to encourage them to become vaccinated.

Source: [https://www.theblaze.com/news/ready-nyt-fauci-admits-to-deceiving-the-public-about-herd-immunity-because-he-wanted-more-people-to-get-vaccinated]

May 28, 2020 – WHO stated that only healthy people caring for sick people should wear face masks.

Source: [https://nypost.com/2020/05/28/healthy-people-should-wear-masks-only-if-caring-for-coronavirus-patients-who-says/].

June 3, 2020 – *NEJM* walks back its April 1, 2020, face mask article information due to media criticism.

Source: [https://www.nejm.org/doi/full/10.1056/NEJMc2020836].

Fake News Media Lied about Face Masks

The fake news mainstream media propagandized face mask usage for healthy people, but infection from asymptomatic carriers is rare, according to WHO doctors.

Source: [https://www.youtube.com/watch?v=NQTBlbx1Xjs].

Instead of reporting factual data and information, fake news does just the opposite. They have raised the face mask hysteria to the point where we have healthy people fighting each other for not wearing face masks. You have ignorant ineffectual governors making face masks mandatory for healthy people to shop and go out.

100,000 Prisoners Released from Jail Due to COVID-19

Across the country, 100,000 prisoners were released to stem the spread of COVID-19 in prisons. My question to these politicians: Well, if face masks work so well in stopping the spread of COVID-19, why didn't these governors and mayors just order these prisoners to wear face masks instead of releasing them from jail?

Transmission of COVID-19 Disease from Asymptomatic Carriers is Rare

WHO held a press conference, and Dr. Maria Van Kerkhove explained the infection rate or the probability of catching COVID-19 from an asymptomatic person is rare.

Source: [https://www.youtube.com/watch?v=NQTBlbx1Xjs].

Legally You Cannot Be Forced to Wear a Face Mask

State governments do not have the authority to issue an order to a private citizen. The governor of a state can issue orders only to state agencies, like the department of health.

The department of health can't issue orders to private citizens; it provides guidance and recommendations. So, the "mandatory" regulation of wearing a face mask is a recommendation. If this guidance or recommendation makes a medical condition worse or causes a problem to your health, you do not have to follow the recommendation of wearing a face mask.

I quote from the New York health department:

> *"You must wear a face mask or face-covering in public when social distancing (staying at least 6 feet apart) is not possible, unless a face covering is not medically tolerated."*

Source: [https://coronavirus.health.ny.gov/system/files/documents/2020/05/13 105_covid-19_facemasks_flyer_050420.pdf].

Further, no government agency is allowed to ask you what medical condition or health issue the face mask is or may be caused because such medical information about yourself is private and protected by federal law.

Is It Worth the Hassle?

If you're entering a store to make a purchase, you technically have the legal right not to wear a face mask. But is it worth the problem it may cause? The store owner probably doesn't know the law, and certainly, the other store patrons don't. I've seen videos where people in a store are practically coming to blows because one person refuses to wear a mask. The fake news media have frightened the public into such a hysteria; they think people not wearing a face mask are putting their lives at risk.

The business owner is required by law to have employees who deal with the public wear a face mask or face legal consequences, like losing his business license. Everyone is reacting to the constant stream of fearmongering misinformation the fake news has been propagating for months.

Mandatory Face Masks at Work

If your employer is forcing you to wear a face mask at work, you can refuse for the legal reasons mentioned above and for violation of OSHA safety standards. Masks decrease oxygen to the blood. OSHA standard 1910.134 states that anything that drops your oxygen level to 19.5 percent is considered oxygen-deficient and in violation. When oxygen sensors are placed between the mouth and mask, there is a significant drop in oxygen. Therefore, you are within your rights to have your employer call an OSHA compliance officer to the firm. The link below is to the OSHA standard I am referencing.

Source: [https://www.osha.gov/laws-regs/standardinterpretations/2007-04-02-0].

19 States Do Not Mandate Masks, Republican Governors Run 18

Source: [https://www.forbes.com/sites/jackbrewster/2020/07/24/19-states-still-dont-mandate-masks-18-are-run-by-republican-governors/#14d8a2f66243].

More Clinical Studies That Prove Wearing Facemasks Are Ineffective Nonsense.

The Association of American Physicians and Surgeons Clinical study conclusion: Wearing masks (other than N95) will not be effective at preventing SARS-CoV-2 transmission, whether worn as source control or as PPE.

Source: [https://aapsonline.org/mask-facts/].

Source: [https://www.nejm.org/doi/full/10.1056/NEJMp2006372?af=R&rss=currentIssue].

Source: [https://pubmed.ncbi.nlm.nih.gov/32203710/].

I can't keep track of how many times the CDC has flip-flopped on the facemask issue. The CDC may flip-flop, but the science remains constant. Below is a CDC study dated 9-11-2020.

CDC STUDY: 85% of COVID-19 patients report 'always' or 'often' wearing a mask – In Other Words, Masks Don't Work

TABLE. Characteristics of symptomatic adults ≥18 years who were outpatients in 11 academic health care facilities and who received positive and negative SARS–CoV–2 test results (N = 314)* — United States, July 1–29, 2020			
	No. (%)		
Characteristic	Case-patients (n = 154)	Control participants (n = 160)	P-value
Reported use of cloth face covering or mask 14 days before illness onset (missing = 2)			
Never	6 (3.9)	5 (3.1)	0.86
Rarely	6 (3.9)	6 (3.8)	
Sometimes	11 (7.2)	7 (4.4)	
Often	22 (14.4)	23 (14.5)	
Always	108 (70.6)	118 (74.2)	

Source: [https://www.cdc.gov/mmwr/volumes/69/wr/mm6936a5.htm].

Facemasks Cause More Problems Than They Solve.

Quote: There is no good evidence that facemasks protect the public against infection with respiratory viruses, including COVID-19. 6

Source: [https://www.ncbi.nlm.nih.gov/pmc/articles/PMC7323223/].

In my opinion, the government forcing you to wear a facemask is its training program in population control, compliance, and obedience - Facemasks are initiated without public consent or scientific validity.

OBEY: Social Distancing

But Social Distancing is a Pseudoscience

SOCIAL DISTANCING

Mandating social distancing for our healthy people population is ridiculous. There are no scientific studies that support social distance.

If someone is sick with the flu or COVID-19, you would expect them to stay home until they recover, not mingling with other people. Naturally, if you see someone sick with the flu or COVID, yes, keep your distance and avoid that person. This is common sense. We don't need the government to mandate common sense. (*Well, maybe liberals do. But I digress.*)

The fact is that these liberal Democrats want a totalitarian nanny state where the government dictates and is intrusive in every part of your life. Not only do these liberal Democrats want to tell you what toilet tissue to buy and how many squares to use, but they also want to tell you what hand you should use to wipe your behind. For example, covid-idiot authoritarian New York Governor Andrew Cuomo constantly mandates asinine laws without common sense. Instead of social distancing, the less than 1 percent of sick people needing to be isolated, he social distanced everyone.

I know what a socialist Democrat would say to this. "Well, what about those asymptomatic people who have COVID-19 and don't know it. They could infect everyone." Not true. According to WHO, these asymptomatic individuals "rarely" infect another person. Remember the Nazi's playbook: "It's for your safety."

The CDC has no peer-reviewed studies because they do not exist. Social distancing is a pseudoscience. Prove this for yourself. Visit the U.S. government's CDC website. There are no "social distancing" studies the CDC can reference. Social distancing, believe it or not, is based on a high school project.

Source: [https://news.abs-cbn.com/spotlight/04/23/20/the-untold-story-of-the-birth-of-social-distancing].

Source: [https://www.telegraph.co.uk/news/2020/06/15/no-scientific-evidence-support-disastrous-two-metre-rule/].

Social distancing as disease control was met with skepticism during the Bush administration when it was conceived. Dr. Scott Gottlieb admitted the draconian measures of social distancing did not work. The expected reduction in COVID-19 infections did not occur in the heavy lockdown states.

Source: [https://amgreatness.com/2020/05/04/the-failed-experiment-of-social-distancing/].

Dr. David Katz predicted the failure of social distancing in his March 20, 2020 article.

Social distancing and isolation in our young low-risk population make the outbreak worse because they inhibit herd immunity.

Source: [https://www.americanthinker.com/articles/2020/05/social_distancing_is_snake_oil_not_science.html].

Source: [https://www.cowen.com/insights/covid-19-discussion-with-dr-david-katz/].

The Democratic Cure for Social Distancing is Rioting

During the lockdown, Democrat governors and mayors arrested and fined anyone who violated their unconstitutional lockdown. If you opened your business, went to work, attended church, or did not obey their public social distancing mandates—like going to the beach and playing with their children at parks, you would be arrested and fined.

Then came the George Floyd Black Lives Matter protests and Antifa. These same Democrat governors and Democrat mayors arrested and fined law-abiding citizens who did not social distance ordered their police departments to stand down during these riots. The police *did not* arrest or fine the people who protested, or the thugs that openly rioted, looted, destroyed public and private property. The mob didn't stop there, they attacked and beat-up innocent people, and some were shot.

And if you defended your home and yourself against the rioting mob, you, not the violent gang, were prosecuted by the Democrats as Mark and Patricia McCloskey, a St. Louis couple, found out.

The leftist media spin was when a business wanted to reopen, or people went outside their homes and didn't social distance or didn't wear a face mask the fake news media labeled them terrorists who threatened public safety.

But the fake news media portrayed the rioting George Floyd protestors and Antifa animals as protestors exercising their first amendment rights, displaying their courage and bravery.

Of course, the rotten cartel of Democrat mayors and Democrat governors followed right along with the fake news media, sanctioned, and defended these lawless rioting animals as "peaceful protestors" exercising their rights. Then the "cancel culture" of Marxist thugs demanded the police be defunded, which several Democrat mayors like NYC mayor Bill De Blasio (AKA Warren Wilhelm Jr.) have agreed to do.

President Donald Trump offered to send in federal forces to stop this rioting in the Democrat-controlled cities. His help was refused. These Democrats' hatred for President Trump is so great they would rather have rioting, looting, businesses burned to the ground, and gun violence than have federal forces come in and stop the rioting.

These riots reflect the Democrat's lawlessness and their outward encouragement of these riots to occur. No Democrat leader in the three months of these violent protests and riots have condemned the rioters. The Democrat response has been and continues to be to defund the police.

To Democrat liberals, **silence is violence, but rioting and looting are okay and justified**.

All I can say to this is that when you vote Democrat, this is the result.

Herd Immunity

There are two ways to prevent being infected with the coronavirus. One is a vaccine, which is months away, and the other is herd immunity.

Herd immunity is when the community of people around you are already immune to the disease. Many people have COVID-19 immunity and don't know it because they became infected with COVID-19 and were asymptomatic. Even if you are asymptomatic, meaning you were infected with COVID-19 with little to no symptoms, one typically associates with the disease, you developed an immunity. Once your body created antibodies to the virus, you are protected from being infected again or infecting other people. When enough people in the population are immune, it's hard for the virus to find a host and infect people who are still vulnerable to the disease.

However, the lockdown inhibits herd immunity from occurring—again, making things worse, not better.

Fake News Called Out

Donald Trump, Jr., accused the Democrats and the media of believing that the coronavirus would kill millions of people so they could use it against his father. They could hope, but a fake pandemic is still manufactured.

It's fair to say that since Trump took office, the stock market had over a hundred positive increases in the last three years. The mainstream media ignored all the positive increments in the stock market, but when the stock market tumbled because of coronavirus fears, that became front-page news.

Neil Ferguson – Breaks Social Distancing Rules

Neil Ferguson, the man who singlehandedly brought about a global lockdown, was forced to resign after breaking his own lockdown rule to meet his married lover. You can't make this stuff up!

Source: [https://redice.tv/news/scientist-behind-failed-coronavirus-models-neil-ferguson-resigns-after-breaking-lockdown-rule-to-meet-his-married-lover].

Democrat Leaders Know It's A Scam, And That's Why They Don't Follow Their Own COVID-19 Rules

Here's a list of Democrat leaders caught breaking their own COVID-19 rules they expect all of us 'common folk' to follow. Keep in mind these are only the ones who got caught. Considering the love affair between legacy media and the Democratic party, I am confident there are more but are covered up.

What you do speaks so loudly that I cannot hear what you say. - Ralph Waldo Emerson

• California Gov. Gavin Newsom,	Democrat
• San Francisco Mayor London Breed,	Democrat
• LA County Supervisor Sheila Kuehl,	Democrat
• Rhode Island Gov. Gina Raimondo,	Democrat
• Michigan Gov. Gretchen Whitmer,	Democrat
• DC Mayor Muriel Bowser,	Democrat
• Illinois Gov. JD Pritzker,	Democrat
• Austin Mayor Steve Adler,	Democrat
• California Rep. Nancy Pelosi,	Democrat
• New York Sen. Chuck Schumer,	Democrat
• Richmond Mayor Lavar Stoney,	Democrat

Source: https://www.mrctv.org/blog/11-government-officials-caught-violating-their-own-covid-rules

Chapter 8: An Example of Incompetence New York Governor's COVID-19 Response

March 20, 2020, Governor Andrew Cuomo locked down NY

Governor Cuomo blundered his way through the COVID-19. His ineptitude wasted hundreds of millions of federal taxpayer dollars having field hospitals built all over New York. The hospitals were not needed or used and were eventually dismantled. He begged President Trump for ventilators; 30,000 were sent to New York, they were not needed or used, and were ultimately shipped to other states.

His health department policies killed thousands of nursing home residents.

Despite these realities, Governor Cuomo shows a complete lack of introspection. He took victory lap after victory lap, complimenting himself on what a great job he has done for New York. Nothing could be further from the truth. Let's examine Gov. Cuomo's response in greater detail.

The Conversion of U.S. States into Banana Republics

Governor Andrew Cuomo (D) invoked emergency powers and took complete authoritarian control over New York and its residents. Cuomo closed schools and businesses he deemed nonessential. I don't understand why the governor considered liquor stores and abortion clinics essential businesses, but not dentists, but this is how banana republics work—no accountability for his decisions.

Killing Seniors in Nursing Homes

Governor Cuomo's health department issued orders instrumental in the deaths of over 11,000 nursing home residents. Cuomo waited six weeks before having his health department rescind the order.

Unfortunately, Governor Cuomo wasn't alone, as the governors across our great nation did the same, converting their states into banana republics with the state governor the *el Presidente* authoritarian ruler.

These New York lockdown measures directly oppose the New York City health department's plan developed for handling the H5N1 pandemic in 2006.

Source: [https://www.documentcloud.org/documents/6820919-NYC-Dept-of-Health-Pandemic-Influenza.html#document/p121].

Look at the following document's yellow highlights. The proper way to handle a pandemic is *not* to institute a lockdown that these state governments enforced.

Isolation of Confirmed/Suspected Cases

Individuals known or believed to be infected with pandemic influenza who are not ill enough to require hospital care will be encouraged to stay home and avoid contact with other persons. Home isolation will be voluntary and guidance will be provided to household members about how to minimize the risk of transmission while caring for the ill person. Mandatory isolation will likely be considered only during the earliest period of a pandemic (see Isolation of Confirmed/Suspected Cases above).

Quarantine of Contacts

Mandatory quarantine of contacts would not be recommended once the pandemic arrives in NYC. Individuals exposed to persons infected with pandemic influenza will be encouraged to be alert for symptoms and to seek medical care if they develop fever and respiratory symptoms. Household members of contacts should pay particular attention to respiratory and hand hygiene practices. Quarantine will only be warranted for a limited time when:

- There is limited disease transmission in the area

- Most cases can be traced to contact with an earlier case or exposure to a known transmission setting (e.g.,a school or workplace where a person has fallen ill)

- Intervention is likely to either significantly slow the spread of infection or to decrease the overall magnitude of an outbreak in the community

Use of Masks in Community Settings

Prevailing evidence suggests that seasonal influenza is primarily spread through droplet transmission. Contact and airborne mechanisms of transmission are thought to play lesser roles. There is a lack of available evidence to suggest that wearing surgical facemasks in community settings by the general public will be beneficial in preventing spread of pandemic influenza.

Health care personnel will be encouraged to wear personal protection equipment (whether surgical facemasks or N95 masks pending federal recommendations) during routine patient care encounters. Patients who are symptomatic with confirmed or suspected pandemic influenza will also be encouraged to wear a surgical facemask during routine health care encounters.

Symptomatic individuals who who must go out in public will be encouraged to wear facemasks. Other actions in reference to facemasks will include:

- A "permissive" approach may be adopted regarding wearing masks in public by individuals who are not ill. At present, neither WHO nor CDC recommends or encourages wearing masks in community settings by people who are well. As information becomes available regarding the primary mode of spread of a pandemic strain, advice regarding wearing masks in public settings may evolve.

- DOHMH plans to purchase and stockpile a supply of facemasks that may be used by the general public as recommended in circumstances described above.

Governor Cuomo's plan for dealing with the COVID-19 threat was complaining of how President Trump was responding to the COVID-19 threat. He criticized how President Trump assessed the COVID-19 threat on a state-by-state basis and offered proportionate federal support. While Cuomo, on the other hand, wanted a one-size-fits-all response.

Trump responded. Cuomo wants "all states to be treated the same. But all states aren't the same. Some are being hit hard by the Chinese virus; some are being hit practically not at all. New York is a very big 'hotspot,' West Virginia has, thus far, zero cases. Andrew, keep politics out of it..."

Had Trump responded in a one-size-fits-all manner that Governor Cuomo recommended, this country would have wasted additional billions of dollars in its COVID-19 response to the states.

I have placed a picture of a chimp on the page. I don't want anyone to misunderstand what I am illustrating; I am not comparing New York Governor Andrew Cuomo to a chimp. I would never insult a defenseless chimp in that manner. Our chimp represents a random decision-maker, like a coin flip. Statistically, our chimp would be correct 50 percent of the time.

So far, Cuomo made a tremendous blunder wanting an equal federal response to all states. Let's continue.

Andrew Cries Wolf

Cuomo's only plan for New York handling the coronavirus threat was to plead for resources from President Donald Trump and the federal government.

On March 27, 2020, Cuomo insisted he needed 40,000 respirators and 140,000 hospital beds based on data and projections.

According to Betsy McCaughey's writing in Real Clear Politics, in 2015, Governor Cuomo was informed by his health department that New York had 16,000 fewer ventilators it would need in a severe pandemic. The ventilators cost $36,000 per unit, making the total cost to purchase 16,000 ventilators $576 million. Governor Cuomo said no. Instead, he asked his health commissioner to develop a plan for rationing the existing ventilators in the event of a pandemic. That rationing plan is what we commonly call a death panel.

Source: [https://www.realclearpolitics.com/articles/2020/03/18/new_yorks_ventilator_rationing_plan_142685.html].

It's not like New York State didn't have the money. Governor Cuomo wasted $750 million in the "Buffalo Billion" solar panel factory quagmire, trying to revitalize the upstate economy. This investment so far has netted approximately 750 new jobs. That works out to about $1 million per job. Good job, governor; imagine what he would do for the country.

Source: [https://nypost.com/2019/08/28/cuomos-buffalo-billion-tainted-tesla-solar-city-faces-audit/].

That's three terrible decisions. How's our chimp looking?

Hospital Beds Delivered to New York

President Trump had the Army Corps build 2,500 beds for field hospitals in the Javits Center in New York City. President Trump also sent our hospital ship, the U.S. Navy's *Comfort*, into New York harbor. This hospital ship has a thousand hospital beds. However, the field hospital and the *USS Comfort* treated only 1,100 patients in three weeks.

Out of the 2,500 beds in the Javits Center, only 145 were used for COVID-19 patients. New York hospitals were never overrun as predicted or even came close to capacity.

Besides this, two more field hospitals were built in Long Island at the State University of New York at Stony Brook and SUNY Old Westbury. These Long Island hospitals cost $270 million to build and were never used for lack of coronavirus patients.

Source: [https://gothamist.com/news/fema-begin-strategic-drawdown-largely-empty-javits-center-and-usns-comfort].

Governor Cuomo was wrong again, big time. But you would never know this by reading the fake news media.

Ventilators

President Trump answered Cuomo's pleas for an additional 30,000 ventilators to add to the 10,000 ventilators New York had in stock. President Trump believed that Cuomo overestimated their need for 40,000 ventilators.

Source: [https://www.syracuse.com/coronavirus/2020/03/president-trump-i-dont-believe-ny-needs-30000-ventilators-for-coronavirus.html].

Cuomo pushed back, asking the Trump administration to "pick the 26,000 people who are going to die."

The fake news mainstream media, always on the Trump attack, called Cuomo's request "fact-based evidence."

President Trump sent over 4,000 additional ventilators to New York. Those additional 4,000 ventilators were never needed or used. The excessive ventilators were eventually shipped from New York to other states.

Governor Cuomo was wrong again. Did the fake news report this? We're up to five wrong decisions.

New York Peaks

New York never needed over 5,000 ventilators at the peak of the coronavirus cases, which the state already had in stock. Another Cuomo failure. **Did you ever hear the mainstream media report that Trump was correct and that Cuomo was wrong?** No, you did not. Instead, you heard nothing but praise from the mainstream media for Democratic Governor Cuomo.

But Wait, There's More! Governor Andrew Cuomo Branded "Killer" Cuomo

Actor James Woods branded Governor Cuomo "Killer Cuomo" for his state directive responsible for killing over 5,000 nursing home residents.

Source: [https://www.breitbart.com/entertainment/2020/05/20/james-woods-brands-new-york-gov-killer-cuomo-over-nursing-home-scandal/].

But this was before it was uncovered the massive undercounting of COVID-19 deaths in the nursing home. The actual total has been up to over 11,000 deaths. It appears NY state had covered up and undercounting nursing home deaths by sending elderly patients to hospitals to die. We'll return to this later.

Cuomo's March 25, 2020, directive ordered the state's nursing homes to accept residents who had been infected with COVID-19 back into the nursing home.

Cuomo's directive caused the coronavirus's spread to our population's most vulnerable and contributed to over 5,000 (really over 11,000) nursing home resident deaths. Keep in mind there were thousands of unused hospital beds in both the Javits Center and the U.S. Navy *Comfort* hospital ship. There was no reason to send infected symptomatic COVID-19 patients back to nursing homes to infect our most vulnerable residents.

On April 23, 2020, after being questioned on the nursing homes deaths and pushback from nursing homes regarding the state's mandate, Cuomo said this during a news conference, "They don't have a right to object. That is the rule, and that is the regulation, and they have to comply with that." Cuomo said further, "If they can't do it, we'll put them in a facility that can do it."

Source: [https://www.rev.com/blog/transcripts/andrew-cuomo-new-york-covid-19-briefing-transcript-april-23].

NEW YORK STATE OF OPPORTUNITY. | # Department of Health

ANDREW M. CUOMO	HOWARD A. ZUCKER, M.D., J.D.	SALLY DRESLIN, M.S., R.N.
Governor	Commissioner	Executive Deputy Commissioner

DATE: March 25, 2020
TO: Nursing Home Administrators, Directors of Nursing, and Hospital Discharge Planners
FROM: New York State Department of Health

Advisory: Hospital Discharges and Admissions to Nursing Homes

Please distribute immediately to:
Nursing Home Administrators, Directors of Nursing, Directors of Social Work, Hospital Discharge Planners

---

COVID-19 has been detected in multiple communities throughout New York State. There is an urgent need to expand hospital capacity in New York State to be able to meet the demand for patients with COVID-19 requiring acute care. As a result, this directive is being issued to clarify expectations for nursing homes (NHs) receiving residents returning from hospitalization and for NHs accepting new admissions.

Hospital discharge planning staff and NHs should carefully review this guidance with all staff directly involved in resident admission, transfer, and discharges.

During this global health emergency, all NHs must comply with the expedited receipt of residents returning from hospitals to NHs. Residents are deemed appropriate for return to a NH upon a determination by the hospital physician or designee that the resident is medically stable for return.

Hospital discharge planners **must** confirm to the NH, by telephone, that the resident is medically stable for discharge. Comprehensive discharge instructions must be provided by the hospital prior to the transport of a resident to the NH.

No resident shall be denied re-admission or admission to the NH solely based on a confirmed or suspected diagnosis of COVID-19. NHs are prohibited from requiring a hospitalized resident who is determined medically stable to be tested for COVID-19 prior to admission or readmission.

Information for healthcare providers on COVID-19 is readily available on the New York State Department of Health public website at https://coronavirus.health.ny.gov/information-healthcare-providers. As always, standard precautions must be maintained, and environmental cleaning made a priority, during this public health emergency.

Critical personal protective equipment (PPE) needs should be immediately communicated to your local Office of Emergency Management, with the appropriate information provided at the time of request. Requests **MUST** include:

o Type and quantity of PPE by size;
o Point of contact at the requesting facility or system;
o Delivery location;
o Date request is needed to be filled by; AND
o Record of pending orders.

Thank you for your ongoing support and cooperation in responding to COVID-19. General questions or comments about this advisory can be sent to covidnursinghomeinfo@health.ny.gov.

Empire State Plaza, Corning Tower, Albany, NY 12237 | health.ny.gov

After causing thousands of deaths, the New York health website deleted Cuomo's health department's March 25, 2020, order. That's why I included it here. On May 10, Cuomo's health department issued a new directive, invalidating his previous mandate.

When asked in a press conference about the March 25 order, Cuomo followed standard liberal procedure: ***if in doubt, just blame Trump, scream, and shout***.

Governor Cuomo falsely claimed he was following federal guidelines re: QSO-20-14-NH. According to Representative Steve Scalise, the Trump administration changed the policies in mid-March to state that nursing home facilities "not prepared" to handle nursing home residents with COVID-19 should not accept such residents.

Source: [https://www.foxnews.com/politics/scalise-governors-coronavirus-nursing-homes].

Source: [https://nypost.com/2020/05/20/gov-cuomo-is-a-hypocrite-on-life-death-and-nursing-homes-devine/].

When blaming Trump failed, Cuomo blamed the nursing homes that followed his March 25, 2020, mandate.

New York lost 59.4 nursing home residents per 1,000 residents. New Jersey Governor Phil Murphy, a Democrat, issued similar orders to the state's nursing homes with even greater catastrophic results—148 residents died per 1,000.

Think about this, while these Democrat governors' idiotic mandates were killing our most vulnerable and elderly citizens in nursing homes, they were also denied visits from any loved ones. They were forcing these nursing home residents to die without family.

I am still keeping count. How's our chimp looking?

In contrast, Florida Governor Ron DeSantis, a Republican, who, as early as March 15, 2020, prohibited the return of coronavirus patients until they were no longer infectious. Florida lost only 11.1 nursing home residents per 1,000.

Cuomo Strikes Again

Cuomo quietly signed legislation in May 2020 shielding and granting immunity to hospitals and nursing homes from any lawsuits stemming from the coronavirus outbreak. Essentially, he just gave immunity to himself.

Consider if a family files a wrongful death suit against a nursing home that knowingly brought in an infected symptomatic COVID-19 patient into their facility, resulting in their family member's death. Any nursing home sued for wrongful death because they followed the governor's March 25 mandate guidelines would file its lawsuit against New York State. So, by granting immunity to the nursing homes, he granted immunity to New York's own health department's mandate. That's killer.

Source: [https://www.theguardian.com/us-news/2020/may/26/andrew-cuomo-nursing-home-execs-immunity].

Cuomo Caught Undercounting Nursing Home Deaths going from 5000 to an estimated 16,000

We have already established 5,000 nursing home deaths, but it appears that it is only a fraction of the real number of nursing home deaths. How do you cover up nursing home deaths? Glad you asked. One step is not to count the casualties of nursing home residents who transferred and died in hospitals. Isn't that "killer"? New York was the only state to do this, which resulted in a massive undercounting.

According to PJ Media, a conservative nursing home death toll is estimated closer to 16,080 deaths. The PJ Media article, see source below, lists all the shenanigans state officials pulled.

Source: [https://pjmedia.com/news-and-politics/matt-margolis/2020/07/27/heres-exactly-how-andrew-cuomo-covered-up-his-deadly-nursing-home-policy-n715550].

Now the Associated Press has also discovered Gov. Cuomo's undercounting. They didn't confirm the estimated 16,000 nursing home death toll, but they did ensure the undercounting is in the thousands.

Source: [https://apnews.com/212ccd87924b6906053703a00514647f].

The result of discovering this undercounting, if accurate, shows that about half the COVID-19 deaths in NY were nursing home deaths directly attributable to Gov. Cuomo's health department mandates.

We can only hope a full investigation is brought to bear on this issue so that the sleight of hand mischief can be exposed and accurate death toll numbers can be assessed.

42% of All COVID-19 Deaths are from Nursing Homes

Forty-two percent of America's coronavirus deaths are nursing home residents.

Source: [https://freopp.org/the-covid-19-nursing-home-crisis-by-the-numbers-3a47433c3f70].

Yet only 1.8 percent of the U.S. population lives in nursing homes.

No Accountability for NY Nursing Home Deaths

Cuomo's health department mandates killed more older adults in nursing homes than died in the 9/11 attacks that brought down the Twin Towers. Where is the outrage? Where is the accountability?

If this had been Trump's fault or Trump's administration, the mainstream fake news media would never stop screeching. The fake news media is just as guilty as Cuomo in these deaths. If they hadn't been screaming "pandemic" hysterically 2.1 billion times in March, perhaps cooler heads would have prevailed, and our resources could have been appropriately applied to the 1.8 percent of our elderly population in nursing homes who needed shelter and quarantine.

We would not have locked down our country's healthy population and would have achieved much better results. But common-sense measures would not have tanked the U.S. economy and weaponized COVID-19 to attack President Trump's reelection.

More Leftist Lunacy

Governor Cuomo released 1,500 inmates from a prison in New York City because of the coronavirus and is surprised violent crime soars: murder, burglary, and auto theft.

Source: [https://www.breitbart.com/politics/2020/04/26/cuomos-new-york-inmate-arrested-rape-days-after-release-jail/].

Governor Cuomo has mandated face mask be worn in public on April 15, 2020. Well, Governor, if face masks work so well, why did you just order all prisoners to wear face masks instead of releasing them from jail?

Source: [https://www.foxnews.com/politics/cuomo-signs-executive-order-requiring-all-new-yorkers-wear-face-masks-coverings-in-public-amid-coronavirus].

Cuomo Twisted Logic Accuses President Trump of Denying Reality

On July 13, 2020, Governor Cuomo accused President Trump of everything he Governor Cuomo is guilty of doing. Is this a total lack of introspection, twisted logic, or a liberal propaganda ploy of "Let's accuse the other side of what we did so they can't throw it back in our face"?

Who's Denying Reality, Governor?

Here's the reality Governor Cuomo is ignoring. Deaths from COVID-19 have flatlined for weeks. Yet he keeps his stranglehold on New York under partial lockdowns.

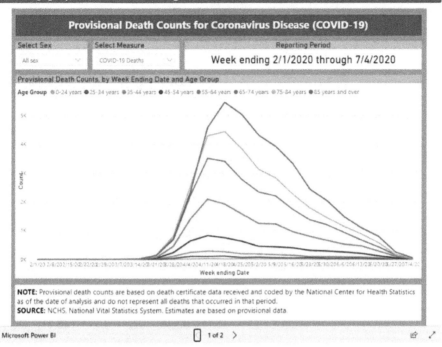

Cuomo's Incompetence

Under Governor Cuomo's leadership (or lack of), New York State leads the country in COVID-19 deaths; over 32,000 people died in New York. The next closest state, New Jersey, has 15,000 deaths.

Cuomo's health department orders that forced nursing homes to accept symptomatic COVID-19 patients into their facilities are directly responsible for thousands of nursing home deaths. Then is caught undercounting COVID-19 nursing home deaths.

Hundreds of millions of federal dollars were wasted to build field hospitals in New York City and New York state for a pandemic that never occurred. The hospitals were dismantled.

We passed "flattening the curve" months ago. Governor Cuomo told New York it would shut down only until the curve was flattened. Another liberal "bait and switch" promise.

Cuomo Criticizes DeSantis

Fake news mainstream media darling New York Governor Cuomo dared to criticize Florida's DeSantis. Here's the tale at the tape July 16, 2020.

State	Population	# of COVID-19 Deaths	Deaths/100,000
NY	19.45M	32,446	169
FL	21M	4,677	22

Nursing Home Deaths May/June 2020

State	Population	# of COVID-19 Deaths	Deaths/1000
NY	101,000	6,000	59.4
FL	72,741	805	11.1
NJ	44,033	6,550	148.8

Source: [https://www.kff.org/other/state-indicator/number-of-nursing-facility-residents/?currentTimeframe=0&sortModel=%7B%22colId%22:%22Location%22,%22sort%22:%22asc%22%7D].

*Above chart does not reflect the massive undercounting of nursing home deaths in NY.

New Jersey Nursing Home Disaster

New Jersey is another nursing home disaster. With 44,033 nursing home residents, Governor Phil Murphy, a Democrat, instituted a similar plan as Cuomo with even greater disastrous results—6,550 nursing home deaths, which works out to 148.8 COVID-19 deaths per 1,000 residents.

Source: [https://covid19.nj.gov/#live-updates].

Cuomo's "Eat to Drink" Mandates

As New York struggles to open up, the governor passed laws that defy common sense, such as the "eat to drink" mandates. Establishments are allowed to serve drinks, but only if selling food is part of the transaction. Establishments quickly learned to circumvent this dopey law by serving tiny portions of food. Some restaurants offered an F.*.C.K. C.U.O.M.O. dollar menu. Rather than see the nonsense of this mandate, Cuomo doubled down and defined what he considered constitutes "food." Chicken wings didn't make the cut, and he threatened to suspend the liquor license of those establishments that did not comply.

Source: [https://www.aier.org/article/ridiculous-liquor-regulations/].

These are not the action of a leader; this is a low middle-level tyrannical bureaucrat drunk with power.

You Don't See Cuomo Living on Unemployment

Cuomo sits in his office, collecting his 200,000 salary as Governor of NY. You don't see Cuomo living on unemployment benefits. Like a government leech nursed on taxpayer money, he has no concept of what's involved in actually working and earning money for a living. He thinks he's essential. My monkey says no. Perhaps if he cut his governor salary and forced himself to live unemployment benefits like the millions of New Yorkers he placed on unemployment by closing their businesses, maybe then he wouldn't be such a COVID-19 dictator.

Cuomo Takes a Victory Lap

Despite Cuomo's incompetent handling of the COVID-19 virus in New York, he took a victory lap, complimenting himself on what a great job he's done. Unbelievable!

Source: [https://www.foxnews.com/media/cnn-jake-tapper-andrew-cuomo-coronavirus-new-york].

Cuomo Writes A Book

Gov. Andrew Cuomo is writing a book on what he believes is his leadership in the COVID-19 scamdemic. Talk about deflection. Gov. Cuomo ought to be writing apologies to the estimated 16,000 families that lost a loved one in a nursing home due to his lack of leadership. Neither Cuomo nor his administration has taken any responsibility for these deaths, and no one is holding them accountable.

Vote Democrat, and these are the results you get. Our chimp says, "Vote for me! Could I be any worse?"

NYC Mayor Bill de Blasio
OBEY: Snitch on Your Neighbor with Mayor Bill

I didn't want to leave out the incompetence of New York City Mayor Bill de Blasio. The mayor started a snitch line that would make the Nazi's proud. Mayor de Blasio encourages people in his video address to photograph and report people not following government social distance guidelines. The mayor told the public that "enforcement is coming right away." Isn't this right out of the Nazi playbook for population control?

Source: NYC Mayor's Office –
[https://www.youtube.com/watch?v=i7Y3TgkSqlo].

Fortunately, many people saw this for what it is and sent the mayor a message, thousands of obscene photos of penises, along with other photographs of Mayor de Blasio himself. I would be hard-pressed to tell them apart. But because of this vital public reaction, the snitch line has been permanently shut down.

Mayor de Blasio released criminals from New York City jails because social distancing couldn't be maintained, then was shocked to learn these released criminals committed additional crimes. NYC's Mayor de Blasio will fine New York City residents $1,000 for walking in the park with their children.

Mayor Bill de Blasio was born Warren Wilhelm, Jr. He worked for the Quixote Center and was a strong supporter of Nicaragua's socialist Marxist government. He joined the Nicaragua political group and held fundraisers to support the Sandinista political party. In 1990 he described himself as an advocate for democratic socialism. He changed his name in 2001 to Bill de Blasio.

Chapter 9: State Governors Drunk with Power

Authoritarians love authoritarianism, and drunk-with-power governors refuse to relinquish the stranglehold they hold on their state.

States Begin Declaring States of Emergencies

February 29, 2020	Washington State Governor Jay Inslee declares a state of emergency in response to the COVID-19 threat.
March 4, 2020	California Governor Gavin Newsom declares a state of emergency in response to the COVID-19 threat.
March 7, 2020	New York Governor Andrew Cuomo declares a state of emergency in response to the COVID-19 threat.
March 9, 2020	New Jersey Governor Phil Murphy declares a state of emergency in response to the COVID-19 threat.
March 9, 2020	Illinois Governor J. B. Pritzker declares a state of emergency in response to the COVID-19 threat.
March 10, 2020	Michigan Governor Gretchen Whitmer declares a state of emergency in response to the COVID-19 threat.

Five States Tanking 33% of U.S. GDP -- Politically Motivated Shutdown Tanking the U.S. Economy

In June 2020, Democratic governors of New York, New Jersey, California, Illinois, and Michigan were still refusing to open their states. These five states account for over one-third of our national GDP.

Source: [https://www.statista.com/statistics/248023/us-gross-domestic-product-gdp-by-state/].

These states are intentionally trying to tank the U.S. economy to destroy President Trump's reelection.

Follow the Science

Follow the science. How many times have I heard that in the last three months? Let me tell you, liberals never follow science unless it coincides with their agenda. Want proof? Ask a liberal when does human life begin? Science will tell you that life begins at the moment of conception.

In any event, there's no such thing as "the science." Sometimes science is a debate between conflicting positions on an issue. If you're fake news, you can politicize "the science" by just reporting the opinion that supports your agenda and ignoring the opposite view as to how fake news reported the threat of COVID-19. There was never "the science," or a consensus supporting the U.S. economy's shutdown or of the draconian measures inflicted upon Americans. There were many educated opposing opinions to the socioeconomic shutdown that were ignored.

Democrat New York Governor Andrew Cuomo, on May 6, 2020, commented about the science from his health department showing the ineffectiveness of the shutdown and shelter-in-place quarantine. The results: 66 percent of new coronavirus hospitalizations are from people who are sheltered at home! Think about this a minute. Their scientific studies show the virus infection spread is more significant in a closed environment, like the home, than outside with casual contact.

Cuomo was shocked by these results. Shocked, I tell you! Maybe if he weren't so cozy with the fake news, this wouldn't have been such a shock. Regardless, authoritarians love authoritarianism, so the scientific facts will not alter that.

Source: [https://www.cnbc.com/2020/05/06/ny-gov-cuomo-says-its-shocking-most-new-coronavirus-hospitalizations-are-people-staying-home.html].

Source: [https://www.medrxiv.org/content/10.1101/2020.02.28.20029272v1].

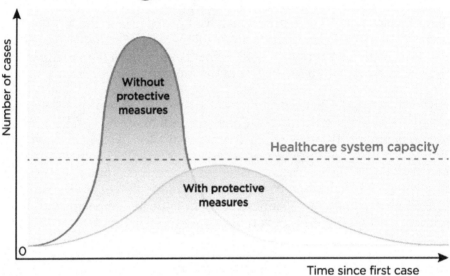

Flattening the Curve of COVID-19

Number of cases (y-axis)

Without protective measures

Healthcare system capacity

With protective measures

Time since first case (x-axis)

Remember Flattening the Curve?

Another liberal sham. Do you remember the lockdown was supposed to last *a few weeks* until we flattened the curve so that hospitals would not be overrun with coronavirus cases? It wasn't even about saving lives. It was so that the hospitals would not be overrun. The models predicting an overflow of our resources and hospitals were wrong. It never occurred. The hospitals were never overrun, and we flattened the curve months ago.

Bait and Switch, Move the Goalposts!

We flattened the curve months ago. But if you flattened the curve, and, as governor, you want to keep your state in lockdown for political reasons, what do you do? Move the goalposts and stay locked down until there is a vaccine for coronavirus. Why stop there? Maybe we should remain in lockdown until the cure for cancer is found too?

These state governors claim they are concerned with the second wave of COVID-19 victims. Really? Why would they be concerned with a second wave when the first wave never arrived?

Some governors are capitalizing on the lockdown.

Virginia Governor Ralph Northam, a Democrat, passed gun control laws that he could not pass when his state was open. When he tried three times, over 20,000 gun owners went to the state capitol to protest, and the bill was killed. So, he passed his gun control during the state lockdown so no one could oppose it. Vote Democrat and this is what you get.

Michigan Governor Gretchen Whitmer, a Democrat, had some residents file two federal lawsuits against the state government for her draconian measures against her state's residents. Governor Whitmer has jailed and fined business owners who violated her state mandates. So far, the governor has lost every legal case that has been brought before the courts.

California Governor Gavin Newsom, a Democrat, is using the lockdown and pandemic too, as he said, "So yes, absolutely we see this as an opportunity to reshape the way we do business and how we govern." He also passed a bill for mail-in voting for the presidential election.

Democrat Governors Kill Nursing Home Residents

Five Democrat governors, Andrew Cuomo from New York, Phil Murphy of New Jersey, Gretchen Whitmer of Michigan, Tom Wolf of Pennsylvania, and Gavin Newsome of California ignored federal guidelines for discharging elderly COVID-19 patients from hospitals to nursing homes.

These five states are responsible for most of the COVID-19 deaths occurring in nursing homes in the country.

Congressman Steve Scalise is leading the investigation asking these governors why they did not follow federal protocols that resulted in over 40,000 nursing home deaths.

If You Live In a State with a Democrat Governor, You Are 2.5X More Likely To Die From Covid-19

	State	Population	Confirmed cases	Deaths	Gov.	Mortality
1	Alaska	731,545	741	12	R	
2	Alabama	4,903,185	29549	838	R	
3	Arizona	7,278,717	50127	1346	R	
4	Arkansas	3,017,804	15142	224	R	
5	Florida	21,477,737	93797	3144	R	
6	Georgia	10,617,423	63809	2642	R	
7	Idaho	1,787,065	4004	89	R	
8	Indiana	6,732,219	42061	2536	R	
9	Iowa	3,155,070	25496	681	R	
10	Maryland	6,045,680	63956	3052	R	
11	Massachusetts	6,892,503	106936	7827	R	
12	Mississippi	2,976,149	20641	938	R	
13	Missouri	6,137,428	18056	965	R	
14	Nebraska	1,934,408	17707	244	R	
15	New Hampshire	1,359,711	5518	339	R	
16	North Dakota	762,062	3251	76	R	
17	Ohio	11,689,100	44261	2697	R	
18	Oklahoma	3,956,971	10038	368	R	
19	South Carolina	5,148,714	23756	644	R	
20	South Dakota	884,659	6225	81	R	
21	Tennessee	6,829,174	34446	524	R	
22	Texas	28,995,881	109581	2183	R	
23	Utah	3,205,958	17068	155	R	
24	Vermont	623,989	1147	56	R	
25	West Virginia	1,792,147	2500	88	R	
26	Wyoming	578,759	1178	20	R	
		Total population 149,514,058		**Total deaths** 31769		0.021 %

	State	Population	Confirmed cases	Deaths	Gov.	Mortality
27	California	39,512,223	175213	5494	D	
28	Colorado	5,758,736	30333	1647	D	
29	Connecticut	3,565,287	45715	4251	D	
30	Delaware	973,764	10681	434	D	
31	Hawaii	1,415,872	789	17	D	
32	Illinois	12,671,821	136104	6625	D	
33	Kansas	2,913,314	12097	256	D	
34	Kentucky	4,467,673	13630	524	D	
35	Louisiana	4,648,794	49385	3104	D	
36	Maine	1,344,212	2938	102	D	
37	Michigan	9,986,857	67545	6087	D	
38	Minnesota	5,639,632	32467	11404	D	
39	Montana	1,068,778	698	20	D	
40	Nevada	3,080,156	12976	486	D	
41	New Jersey	8,882,190	168834	12924	D	
42	New Mexico	2,096,829	10430	466	D	
43	New York	19,453,561	387272	31083	D	
44	North Carolina	10,488,084	51390	1215	D	
45	Oregon	4,217,737	6572	188	D	
46	Pennsylvania	12,801,989	85590	6419	D	
47	Rhode Island	1,059,361	16337	894	D	
48	Virginia	8,535,519	57443	1607	D	
49	Washington	7,614,893	28225	1265	D	
50	Wisconsin	5,822,434	24539	744	D	
		Total population = 178,019,716		**Total deaths** = 97256		0.054 %

Sourced: *June 22, 2020*

Sources: https://www.foxnews.com/health/coronavirus-in-us-state-by-state-breakdown

Florida and Georgia Ease the Lockdown

When Florida and Georgia eased their lockdown restrictions, the fake news mainstream media attacked. The models said to prepare for a rise in coronavirus cases. Just the opposite occurred. Florida cases declined by 14 percent, and Georgia cases declined by 12 percent.

Source: [https://www.axios.com/coronavirus-cases-map-high-risk-states-8ceeaa05-cc07-4e8b-b9f4-df3a3315f143.html].

Florida Republican Governor Ron DeSantis said, "There's been a lot that's been done to try to promote fear, to promote worst-case scenarios, to drive hysteria." He continued, "People should know that worst-case scenario thinking has not proven to be true."

Fake News Media Spin

If you listen to the fake news media, Cuomo is doing a great job, and Florida's governor is putting his state residents at risk. You can't make this stuff up, except if you're fake news.

Easing Lockdown Results in Increased COVID-19 Cases

As the lockdowns eased and people mingled, there was an increase in COVID-19 cases. This is to be expected. The fake news media is spinning this information like a top. They are promoting the growth in COVID-19 cases as a failure. It is not; here's why.

The fake news is not telling you that the increase in COVID-19 cases does not result in a proportional increase in hospitalizations or deaths. Why? Because the rise in COVID-19 cases is with young, healthy people. These healthy people are our low-risk population.

Remember, close to 50 percent of people who become infected don't even know it.

Once the low-risk population has been infected, they are immune. When you are immune, you are no longer a carrier for the disease. When enough of the population becomes immune, the disease doesn't have the carriers to infect the still-vulnerable people. They call this herd immunity. Easing the lockdowns in Florida and the increase in cases in the low-risk population is building herd immunity.

COVID-19 Lockdowns Doesn't Suspend Our Constitutional Rights.

The courts are siding with citizens who are fighting the state's unlawful and prolonged lockdown. For example, here is a quote from Justice James Blacklock from the Texas Supreme Court:

"The Constitution is not suspended when the government declares a state of disaster." In re Abbott, №20–0291, 2020 WL 1943226, at *1 (Texas, April 23, 2020): "All government power in this country, no matter how well-intentioned, derives only from the state and federal constitutions. Government power cannot be exercised in conflict with these constitutions, even in a pandemic."

Source: [https://www.txcourts.gov/media/1446506/200340c.pdf].

Courts Overturning Lockdowns

The courts in Wisconsin, Oregon, and Ohio have overturned the state's lockdowns. The courts have concluded the states are overreaching their public health power.

In Wisconsin, the courts decided that Andrea Palm, a Democrat running the Wisconsin Department of Health, did not have the power to close businesses, force residents to stay home under house arrest, or threaten citizens with jail and fines for violations.

"If we tolerate unconstitutional government orders during an emergency, whether out of expediency or fear, we abandon the Constitution at the moment we need it most. Any government that has made the grave decision to suspend the liberties of a free people during a health emergency should welcome the opportunity to demonstrate—both to its citizens and to the courts—that its chosen measures are absolutely necessary to combat a threat of overwhelming severity. The government should also be expected to

demonstrate that less restrictive measures cannot adequately address the threat." – Justice Blacklock.

Source: [https://www.txcourts.gov/media/1446506/200340c.pdf].

In Ohio, Judge Eugene Lucci stated Ohio's health department did not meet the legal requirements to restrict a healthy individuals' movements or activities. A "quarantine" is supposed to last only two to fourteen days.

Whenever a citizen fought back against the state's lockdown, the citizen has won. Unfortunately, this hasn't stopped the states from enforcing their lockdown mandates.

Chapter 10: Not Enough People Are Dying

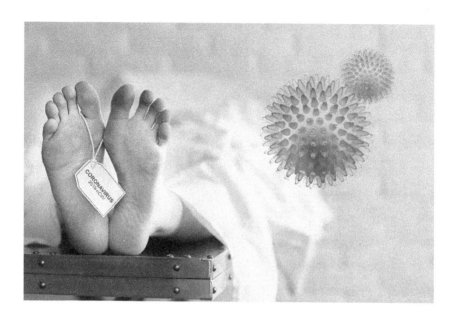

What Happens If You Called a Pandemic and Not Enough People Died?
Now It's a Crisis!

Considering the economic and mental anguish the lockdowns have caused across the country, not having enough people succumb to COVID-19 and die is a problem. You have a few federal agencies, the NIH, the CDC, every state government, and governor who initiated lockdowns, Democrat leaders who weaponized COVID-19, and the mainstream media press with a vested interest.

Source: [https://www.lewrockwell.com/2020/05/no_author/the-dubious-covid-models-the-tests-and-now-the-consequences/].

Source: [https://www.theblaze.com/news/former-ny-times-reporter-sounds-alarm-over-flawed-coronavirus-models].

In New York, there wasn't a health system crisis. President Trump responded to Governor Cuomo pleading for beds and respirators by building field hospitals with thousands of beds in New York City, sending the hospital ship into New York harbor, and issuing thousands of ventilators to New York. None of these beds and supplies were needed or used.

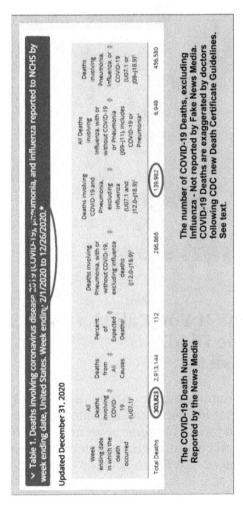

Reference: [https://www.cdc.gov/nchs/nvss/vsrr/covid19/index.htm].

Pumping Up the Pandemic

The mainstream news media continues to report exaggerated COVID-19 deaths. The CDC keeps numerous statistics. The death number used by the mainstream media includes influenza deaths with COVID-19 or without COVID-19.

- All COVID-19 deaths are intentionally inflated because the CDC changed its standing seventeen-year reporting procedure for filling out death certificates. The brand-new guidelines for COVID-19 changed the comorbidities procedure. Had the CDC not changed its comorbidities procedure, it is estimated that reported COVID-19 deaths would be reduced by more than 90 percent. The CDC reports that only 6% of the reported COVID-19 Deaths are from COVID-19 alone.

CDC States - Only 6% of the reported COVID-19 deaths are from COVID-19 by itself!

Comorbidities

Table 3 shows the types of health conditions and contributing causes mentioned in conjunction with deaths involving coronavirus disease 2019 (COVID-19). For 6% of the deaths, COVID-19 was the only cause mentioned. For deaths with conditions or causes in addition to COVID-19, on average, there were 2.6 additional conditions or causes per death. The number of deaths with each condition or cause is shown for all deaths and by age groups. For data on comorbidities, ⟳ Click here to download.

Source https://www.cdc.gov/nchs/nvss/vsrr/covid_weekly/index.htm

John Hopkins Reports Relatively No Additional Deaths in 2020 Due to COVID-19

On **Nov. 22, 2020**, John Hopkins published this truthful report. It created such a "liberal" furor that John Hopkins had to retract and delete the report from its website. Another example of "Cancel Culture" intimidation and fact censoring.

From the original John Hopkins report:

> *Surprisingly, the deaths of older people stayed the same before and after COVID-19. Since COVID-19 mainly affects the elderly, experts expected an increase in the percentage of deaths in older age groups. However, this increase is not seen from the CDC data. In fact, the*

percentages of deaths among all age groups remain relatively the same.

Transfer of Deaths

If you look at the death toll numbers for other causes of death, they all decreased in proportion to the deaths reported for COVID-19

From the original John Hopkins report:

This trend is completely contrary to the pattern observed in all previous years. Interestingly, as depicted in the table below, the total decrease in deaths by other causes almost exactly equals the increase in deaths by COVID-19. This suggests, according to Briand, that the COVID-19 death toll is misleading. Briand believes that deaths due to heart diseases, respiratory diseases, influenza, and pneumonia may instead be recategorized as being due to COVID-19.

Source: [https://www.thegatewaypundit.com/2020/11/johns-hopkins-study-mysteriously-disappears-shows-spite-covid-no-deaths-2020-prior-years].

Source: [https://pjmedia.com/news-and-politics/matt-margolis/2020/11/27/johns-hopkins-study-saying-covid-19-has-relatively-no-effect-on-deaths-in-u-s-deleted-after-publication-n1178930].

Wayback Machine Link to Original Study Source:
[https://web.archive.org/web/20201126223119/https://www.jhunewsletter.com/article/2020/11/a-closer-look-at-u-s-deaths-due-to-covid-19].

The John Hopkins report appears to support the CDC's fact that only 6% of reported COVID-19 deaths are from COVID-19 by itself. If there aren't over 300,000 + excessive deaths in the US, there can't be an excess of 300,000 deaths due to COVID-19 as the liberal legacy media and their brainwashed followers continually repeat. There is a big difference between dying with COVID-19 and dying from COVID-19.

CDC and Death Certificate Manipulation

The government's method to boost COVID-19 death toll numbers is to classify any death as a coronavirus death, as long as the person who died was found to be infected with the coronavirus.

To change the "death certificate" methodology to boost COVID-19 death, the CDC needed to implement and send out new guidelines to hospitals and doctors across the country. I have copies of the guidelines sent out on March 4 and March 24.

According to the guidelines: a person in a head-on car collision, who died on the scene and tested positive for the coronavirus in the morgue, their death was counted as a COVID-19 death. The same is true for heart attacks, strokes, etc. See excerpt below.

Guidance for Certifying COVID-19 Deaths
March 4, 2020

guidance. It is important to emphasize that **Coronavirus Disease 2019** or **COVID-19** should be reported on the death certificate for all decedents where the disease caused or is assumed to have caused or contributed to death. Other terminology, e.g.,

Dr. Annie Bukacek is a Montana physician with over thirty years of medical experience and has a seat on a Montana county health department board. She blew the whistle on the CDC death certificate guidelines that inflate COVID-19 deaths.

Source: [https://www.youtube.com/watch?v=WZDy2lMJ-g0].

Dr. Bukacek states in the video how the CDC guidelines force doctors to inflate COVID-19 deaths.

CDC Guidelines – Full Document March 4

National Vital Statistics System

Guidance for Certifying COVID-19 Deaths
March 4, 2020

NCHS is receiving questions about how deaths involving the new coronavirus strain should be reported on death certificates. We are working on formal guidance to certifiers to be published as soon as possible. In the meantime, to address the immediate need, here is some basic information that can be shared in advance of the more formal and detailed guidance. It is important to emphasize that **Coronavirus Disease 2019** or **COVID-19** should be reported on the death certificate for all decedents where the disease caused or is assumed to have caused or contributed to death. Other terminology, e.g., SARS-CoV-2, can be used as long as it is clear that it indicates the 2019 coronavirus strain, but we would prefer use of WHO's standard terminology, e.g., COVID-19. Specification of the causal pathway leading to death in Part I of the certificate is also important. For example, in cases when COVID-19 causes pneumonia and fatal respiratory distress, both pneumonia and respiratory distress should be included along with COVID-19 in Part I. Certifiers should include as much detail as possible based on their knowledge of the case, medical records, laboratory testing, etc. If the decedent had other chronic conditions such as COPD or asthma that may have also contributed, these conditions can be reported in Part II. Here is an example:

CAUSE OF DEATH (See instructions and examples)		Approximate Interval Onset to death
32. **PART I.** Enter the chain of events—diseases, injuries, or complications—that directly caused the death. DO NOT enter terminal events such as cardiac arrest, respiratory arrest, or ventricular fibrillation without showing the etiology. DO NOT ABBREVIATE. Enter only one cause on a line. Add additional lines if necessary		
IMMEDIATE CAUSE (Final disease or condition resulting in death) → a. Due to (or as a consequence of):	Acute respiratory distress syndrome	2 days
Sequentially list conditions, if any, leading to the cause listed on line a. Enter the **UNDERLYING CAUSE** (disease or injury that initiated the events resulting in death) **LAST** b. Due to (or as a consequence of):	Pneumonia	10 days
c. Due to (or as a consequence of):	COVID-19	10 days
d.		
PART II. Enter other significant conditions contributing to death but not resulting in the underlying cause given in PART I.	33. WAS AN AUTOPSY PERFORMED? ☐ Yes ■ No	
	34. WERE AUTOPSY FINDINGS AVAILABLE TO COMPLETE THE CAUSE OF DEATH? ☐ Yes ☐ No	
35. DID TOBACCO USE CONTRIBUTE TO DEATH? ☐ Yes ☐ Probably ■ No ☐ Unknown	36. IF FEMALE ■ Not pregnant within past year ☐ Pregnant at time of death ☐ Not pregnant, but pregnant within 42 days of death ☐ Not pregnant, but pregnant 43 days to 1 year before death ☐ Unknown if pregnant within the past year	37. MANNER OF DEATH ■ Natural ☐ Homicide ☐ Accident ☐ Pending Investigation ☐ Suicide ☐ Could not be determined

For more general guidance and training on cause-of-death reporting, certifiers can be referred to the Cause of Death mobile app available through https://www.cdc.gov/nchs/nvss/mobile-app.htm and the Improving Cause of Death Reporting online training module, which can be found at https://www.cdc.gov/nchs/nvss/improving_cause_of_death_reporting.htm.

Steven Schwartz, PhD
Director – Division of Vital Statistics
National Center for Health Statistics
3311 Toledo Rd | Hyattsville, MD 20782

New Coding Procedures for COVID-19 to Increase Fatalities

The CDC already had established guidelines for reporting fatalities: the **2003** – CDC Medical Examiners' and Coroners' Handbook on Death Registration. The CDC threw out the book and devised new procedures for reporting COVID-19 deaths. These new procedures were issued on March

4 and March 24, 2020. The March 4 directive told doctors to report COVID-19 on the death certificates, where COVID-19 "caused or is *assumed* to have caused or contributed to death."

No Positive Test Required to Declare COVID-19 as Cause of Death

The "assumed" is a big deal, when the U.S. government motivates hospitals with additional money to classify deaths as COVID-19 deaths. Below is an excerpt from the March 24, 2020, guidelines.

Should "COVID-19" be reported on the death certificate only with a confirmed test?
COVID-19 should be reported on the death certificate for all decedents where the disease caused **or is assumed to have caused or contributed to death**. Certifiers should include as much detail as possible based on their knowledge of the case, medical records, laboratory testing, etc. If the decedent had other chronic conditions such as COPD or asthma that may have also contributed, these conditions can be reported in Part II. (See attached Guidance for Certifying COVID-19 Deaths)

Steven Schwartz, PhD
Director – Division of Vital Statistics
National Center for Health Statistics
3311 Toledo Rd | Hyattsville, MD 20782

Here the CDC confirms again, and I'm quoting from their guidelines, see image above that "COVID-19 should be reported on the death certificate for all decedents where is the disease caused **or is assumed to have caused or contributed to death.**"

According to the guidelines, car accidents and gunshot wounds to the head should be classified and counted as COVID-19 deaths, and they are. Positive tests for COVID-19 are not required to declare COVID-19 as the cause of death on a death certificate; it can be assumed.

The CDC implemented this brand new "made up" Death Certificate guidelines just for COVID-19. It has inflated COVID-19 deaths by more than 900%. That's some inflation factor!

Source: [https://childrenshealthdefense.org/news/if-covid-fatalities-were-90-2-lower-how-would-you-feel-about-schools-reopening/].

Senator Scott Jensen, MD, of Minnesota Confirms

Senator Scott Jensen, MD, a Minnesota Republican, confirmed this death certificate manipulation. He explained on numerous shows how the CDC coached doctors to declare COVID-19 as a factor in the causation of death without a COVID-19 test.

Source: [https://www.thegatewaypundit.com/2020/04/huge-mn-senator-dr-reveals-hhs-document-coaching-overcount-covid-19-cases-copy-document-video/].

Source: [https://www.foxnews.com/media/physician-blasts-cdc-coronavirus-death-count-guidelines].

Incentivize Hospitals

One way to boost COVID-19 infection and patient numbers are to reward hospitals to classify patients as coronavirus patients.

$5,000 per Medicare patient

$13,000 per coronavirus patient

$39,000 per patient on a ventilator

Source: [https://thespectator.info/2020/04/09/hospitals-get-paid-more-to-list-patients-as-covid-19-and-three-times-as-much-if-the-patient-goes-on-ventilator-video/?utm_source=wnd&utm_medium=wnd&utm_campaign=syndicated].

Source: [https://www.usatoday.com/story/news/factcheck/2020/04/24/fact-check-medicare-hospitals-paid-more-covid-19-patients-coronavirus/3000638001/].

Ventilators Can Kill

Source:[https://articles.mercola.com/sites/articles/archive/2020/05/06/adverse-effects-of-mechanical-ventilation.aspx?cid_source=dnl&cid_medium=email&cid_content=art1HL&cid=20200506Z1&et_cid=DM527824&et_rid=865893445&fbclid=IwAR0BdJShfAnLooOL7bsOZ2knOPY43j7PgagBWe6x92bfb8rQfAOsir26jiQ].

Ventilators are Overused with COVID-19 Patients

Source: [https://www.statnews.com/2020/04/08/doctors-say-ventilators-overused-for-covid-19/].

But Wait, There's More!

As COVID-19 testing proceeds across the country, more people are testing positive and have COVID-19 antibodies than anyone thought possible. The last ranges are 33 percent to 45 percent of positive tests for asymptomatic people but have COVID-19. Meaning anyone in this group who dies can be classified as a COVID-19 death because they can test positive for COVID-19. Anyone who recovers from COVID-19 and dies later for an unrelated issue can also be classified as a COVID-19 death.

As of July 2, 2020, the CDC reported 35 million people had been tested. Out of that, 3,223,047 tested positive. That's 3,223,047 potential COVID-19 deaths just waiting to be tallied.

However, a positive test result could just be reading antibodies you developed from having another coronavirus called a cold. So, what good are all these tests?

How to get an antibody test

Decisions about testing are made by state or local ☐ health departments or healthcare providers.

Antibody tests for COVID-19 are available through healthcare providers and laboratories. Check with your healthcare provider to see if they offer antibody tests and whether you should get one.

Guidance on Interpreting COVID-19 Test Results ☐ ☐ : A guide for understanding test results and determining what actions to take.

What do your results mean?

If you test positive

- A positive test result shows you may have antibodies from an infection with the virus that causes COVID-19. However, there is a chance a positive result means that you have antibodies from an infection with a virus from the same family of viruses (called coronaviruses), such as the one that causes the common cold.

Source: [https://www.cdc.gov/coronavirus/2019-ncov/testing/serology-overview.html].

Real COVID-19 Death Toll

We will never know the real death toll because the U.S. government and CDC implemented death certificate procedures and hospital incentives to inflate COVID-19 deaths.

The only rationale I can think of for such inappropriate number counting to inflate the COVID-19 death numbers is to justify and possibly maintain the lockdowns across the country, push for mandatory vaccinations (when a vaccine becomes available), and force "mail-in voting" to cheat the Presidential election.

Did You Hear the Latest?

I'm beginning to hear the drumbeat of a mutated or variant form of the COVID-19 virus. Wow, just in time to re-create another virus Pandemic to keep everyone locked down now that we have a vaccine for the original COVID-19 China Virus.

Chapter 11: Did Lockdowns Work?

The Lockdowns Failed at Every Level

The lockdowns did not cause an appreciable halt in the spread of the COVID-19 virus. The COVID-19 death prediction models were incorrect and grossly inflated.

The lockdown will cost more lives than it saved. There will be more deaths caused by the lockdown in the next decade than has been caused by the COVID-19 virus.

JP Morgan Study Shows Lockdowns Are Ineffective
Didn't Affect COVID-19 Pandemic

According to published information from JP Morgan's Quantitative and Derivative Strategy, the lockdowns across the country are ineffective. The JP Morgan data agree and corroborates the non-lockdown approach taken by Sweden.

The reality is contrary to the fake news prediction propaganda. Extrapolating the study's information illustrates that the socioeconomic shutdown and the resulting spending of trillions of dollars in stimulus packages were unnecessary.

Source: [https://www.dailymail.co.uk/news/article-8347635/Lockdowns-failed-alter-course-pandemic-JP-Morgan-study-claims.html].

Source: [https://dailycaller.com/2020/05/20/jp-morgan-infection-rates-decreasing-states-that-ended-lockdowns/].

Source: [https://www.thenewamerican.com/usnews/politics/item/35797-jp-morgan-study-covid-lockdowns-ineffective-millions-of-livelihoods-being-destroyed-for-nothing].

Source: [https://www.dailymail.co.uk/news/article-8347901/US-states-LOWER-infection-rates-lockdowns-end-study-claims.html].

Hundreds of Thousands Will Die Because Of The Lockdown

Hundreds of thousands of lives and millions of years of life will be lost because of the lockdown. Far more than the death toll of COVID-19. Don't believe it? Let's start breaking it down.

Cancer

On average, 150,000 new cancer cases are discovered each month in the US. Because many hospitals have shut down screening and diagnostics, we will see an upswing in cancer deaths in the next few years. One estimate has 60,000 cancer deaths will become attributed to the lockdown because of delayed diagnosis and treatment.

Source: [https://www.itv.com/news/2020-04-22/60-000-cancer-patients-could-die-because-of-lack-of-treatment-or-diagnosis-oncologist-on-coronavirus-dilemma/].

Also, there are currently 650,000 patients receiving chemotherapy. Approximately half have missed their treatments. Missed treatments will increase the mortality of cancer patients undergoing chemotherapy. Is anyone checking this increase in mortality?

Strokes

Emergency stroke evaluations are down 40%.

Domestic Abuse has Risen Globally

Source: [https://www.nytimes.com/2020/04/06/world/coronavirus-domestic-violence.html].

Governor Cuomo's responded to reporters regarding the increase in domestic violence and suicides. Cuomo said they are worth the price of the coronavirus lockdown. I think Andrew may have had a different opinion if he were the one "sheltered at home" being beaten every day by an abusive parent or spouse.

Source: [https://www.thegatewaypundit.com/2020/04/ny-gov-cuomo-suicides-increased-domestic-violence-worth-price-coronavirus-lockdown-save-life-video/].

Alcoholism and Relapse

Also, 150,000 deaths from alcoholism, drug abuse, and suicide over the next decade directly resulted in the COVID-19 coronavirus lockdown.

Source: [https://www.usatoday.com/story/news/health/2020/05/08/coronavirus-pandemic-boosts-suicide-alcohol-drug-death-predictions/3081706001/].

Drug Overdoses Increases

The pre-COVID-19 monthly deaths from a drug overdose were 680. Since COVID-19, the deaths from drug overdoses have increased to 2,348 deaths per month.

Source: [https://www.aier.org/article/lockdowns-are-killing-young-adults/]

Unemployment Increases Mortality

With unemployment at 36 million, it translates to an additional 7,200 lives lost per month.

Source: [https://nypost.com/2020/04/20/explaining-the-link-between-unemployment-deaths-amid-coronavirus/].

Source: [https://news.yale.edu/2002/05/23/rising-unemployment-causes-higher-death-rates-new-study-yale-researcher-shows].

Lost Income

Statistically, every 17 million dollars lost in U.S. income results in one additional death. This translates into 65,000 deaths each month of the economic shutdown.

Source: [https://thehill.com/opinion/healthcare/499394-the-covid-19-shutdown-will-cost-americans-millions-of-years-of-life].

Source: [https://www.acsh.org/news/2020/05/27/coronavirus-lockdown-costing-more-lives-its-saving-14815].

Keeping Count?

Are you keeping count? So far, these are only domestic deaths in the United States. You would have to extrapolate these numbers to all the affected nations globally to gauge the full impact.

200,000 Could Die in the U.K. Because of Lockdown

Source: [https://www.dailymail.co.uk/news/article-8539541/200-000-people-die-delays-healthcare-report-warns.html].

10,000 Children Starve To Death Each Month Because of Global Lockdown

Source: [https://www.huffpost.com/entry/coronavirus-hunger-child-deaths_n_5f1f7e9ac5b638cfec48e471].

Still, counting?

Again, this is only a fraction of the deaths that will be attributed to the lockdowns globally. If there is an excessive death for the year 2020in the US, how many of those deaths can be attributed to the COVID-19 lockdowns and not from COVID-19?

How about States that Didn't Lockdown?

Some states have a lax lockdown or no lockdown at all on their businesses and residents. These states have fared far better than the states that instituted tyrannical lockdowns. Data as of July 2, 2020.

- Arkansas   Gov. Asa Hutchinson (R)   281 Covid-19 Deaths
- Iowa   Gov. Kim Reynolds (R)   721 Covid-19 Deaths
- Nebraska   Gov. Pete Ricketts (R)   284 Covid-19 Deaths
- North Dakota   Gov. Doug Burgum (R)   80 Covid-19 Deaths
- South Dakota   Gov. Kristi Noem (R)   97 Covid-19 Deaths
- Utah   Gov. Gary Herbert (R)   181 Covid-19 Deaths
- Wyoming   Gov. Mark Gordon (R)   20 Covid-19 Deaths

You may have noticed a trend. The states above all have Republican governors.

In contrast, let's compare these to an equal number of states with an oppressive lockdown and highest COVID-19 deaths.

U.S. States that Lockdown with Highest COVID-19 Deaths (July 2, 2020)

- New York   Gov. Andrew Cuomo (D)   32,043 Covid-19 Deaths
- New Jersey   Gov. Phil Murphy (D)   15,078 Covid-19 Deaths
- Massachusetts   Gov. Charlie Baker (R)   8,053 Covid-19 Deaths
- Illinois   Gov. J.B. Pritzker (D)   6,951 Covid-19 Deaths
- Pennsylvania   Gov. Tom Wolf (D)   6,684 Covid-19 Deaths
- Michigan   Gov. G. Whitmer (D)   6,198 Covid-19 Deaths
- California   Gov. Gavin Newsom (D)   6,169 Covid-19 Deaths

You may have noticed another trend. The highest COVID-19 deaths occur in states with Democrat governors in charge.

No-Lockdown Countries

Sweden

Sweden never locked down and never experienced the predicted COVID-19 outbreak, nor the 96,000 deaths predicted by the models. It has fared far better than many countries, like the United Kingdom, that implemented the draconian emergency measures. On June 2, 2020, Neil Ferguson admitted that Sweden achieved the same or better results than the U.K., without resorting to draconian restrictions.

Source: [https://dnyuz.com/2020/06/02/prof-lockdown-neil-ferguson-admits-sweden-used-same-science-as-uk-but-has-suppressed-coronavirus-without-tough-restrictions/].

Source: [https://www.dailywire.com/news/epidemiologist-who-triggered-worldwide-lockdowns-admits-without-instituting-full-lockdown-sweden-essentially-getting-same-effect?itm_source=parsely-api].

Let's see how Sweden fared compared to other countries that imposed draconian lockdowns on its citizens. Data dated July 2, 2020.

Country	Population	Lockdown	COVID-19 Total Deaths	COVID-19 Deaths/100,000
Sweden	10M	N	5,400	53.7
UK	67.8M	Y	44,100	65.1
Spain	47.3M	Y	28,300	60.7
France	65.2M	Y	29,800	45.8
Italy	60.4M	Y	34,800	57.6

Countries That Did Not Lockdown

Japan	126.4M	N	977	0.8
Belarus	9.7M	N	418	4.3
Taiwan	23.5M	N	7	0.03

How we did in New York

NYC	8.3M	Y	18,555	223.5
NYS	19.45M	Y	37,137	191.4

The above chart proves that not locking down a country didn't start the "predicted" pandemic. As noted above, Neil Ferguson, June 2, 2020, admitted that Sweden achieved the same or better results than the U.K. without resorting to draconian restrictions.

Japan

Japan's state of emergency never included locking down its citizens or businesses, and despite all the editorial handwringing with "experts" expecting Japan to explode with coronavirus outbreaks, it never occurred.

Japan's Prime Minister Shinzo Abe ended his country's state of emergency on May 25, 2020.

Japan has a population of 126 million people. As of July 2, 2020, approximately 19,282 cases of COVID-19 were reported, and only 944 had died.

Taiwan

Taiwan never locked down, and out of a population of 23 million had only 446 cases and seven deaths. How did Taiwan avoid coronavirus infections and fatalities? Primarily it was a healthy distrust of China and WHO to report truthful facts. Taiwan tried to warn both China and WHO of human-to-human transfer of the virus in December 2019.

Norway Realizes Its Mistake

Norway's health chief Camilla Stoltenberg now believes the lockdowns weren't necessary. She stated on May 22, 2020, that "Norway could have controlled infection without lockdown."

Source: [https://www.thelocal.no/20200522/norway-could-have-controlled-infection-without-lockdown-health-chief].

Source: [https://townhall.com/tipsheet/mattvespa/2020/05/26/norwegian-health-chief-we-could-have-controlled-infection-without-a-lockdown-n2569471].

This is the kind of honesty and transparency lacking in the American government.

600 Doctors Petition President Trump to End the Lockdown

The lockdown is doing more damage to our health and economy. On May 19, 2020, 600 doctors signed and sent a petition to President Trump to end the states' illegal lockdown for national health reasons.

Source: [https://www.foxnews.com/politics/doctors-raise-alarm-about-health-effects-of-continued-coronavirus-shutdown].

Economic Devastation – 40 Million Unemployed

The number of Americans on unemployment was 23 million, or 14.7 percent, as of April 2020, but this number has since risen to over 40 million unemployment claims.

Source: U.S. Bureau of Labor Statistics.

That's only part of the story. Businesses that have shut down and can never reopen are not counted. The trillions of dollars in debt we have incurred to support companies and individuals are not shown in any graph.

The government has made unemployment so attractive by implementing a $600 a week bonus in addition to standard unemployment, and workers are incentivized not to return to work. Is this the plan of the Democrats to convince people to shelter at home?

Incentivized Unemployment – Stay at Home

A part-time worker in New York City I know was making $150 per week while working is now collecting $105 in unemployment plus $600 from the federal government, for a total of $705 per week. Why go back to work? The $600-a-week bonus on unemployment ends in July 2020.

Source: [https://www.cnn.com/2020/03/25/politics/senate-stimulus-unemployment-benefits-coronavirus/index.html].

Source: [https://www.businessinsider.com/stimulus-package-unemployment-benefits-increase-2020-3?op=1].

Economic Devastation

The economic devastation this country is undergoing is just at the beginning. There is no free lunch. The government doesn't make money; it only collects money. It collects money from taxpayers. So, while the feds are spending trillions of dollars of stimulus money into the economy to appease people and businesses, that money must eventually be paid back, paid back by us, the taxpayers. The payback may include inflation and a higher cost of living (food, gas, goods) with long-term static wages, which will lower the "middle class" standard of living for Americans.

U.S. Government Wastes $660 Million for Empty Hospitals

All across the United States, field hospitals were constructed to meet the demands of coronavirus victims. The hospital beds laid empty, waiting for coronavirus pandemic victims who never arrived. The field hospitals are being removed, but our cost will never disappear. Unfortunately, this is just a small portion of the trillions of dollars lost in the United States for the fake pandemic.

Chapter 12: Hydroxychloroquine, an Example of Media Censorship

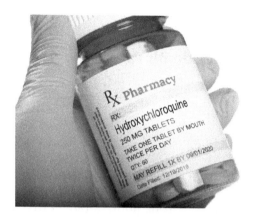

Ever since President Trump mentioned the antimalaria drug hydroxychloroquine combined with azithromycin as a potential game-changer in the treatment of COVID-19, the fake news mainstream media have gone into a feeding frenzy to discredit both the drug and Trump. Some phony news headlines called it "False Hope," "Misguided," "Reckless," and question a profit motive for promoting the potential use of this drug.

Another example of the fake news mainstream media politicizing science and attempting to discredit a widely used drug as quackery, it is a medicine used successfully for over fifty years. Why? Because Donald Trump recommended it to be studied. Or, is there more to it?

First, let's look at how the mainstream media reported on hydroxychloroquine.

Washington Post's fact-checker analysis called it "False Hope."

Source: [https://www.washingtonpost.com/politics/2020/04/13/how-false-hope-spread-about-hydroxychloroquine-its-consequences/].

CNN: "greater risk of death"

Source:
[https://www.cnn.com/2020/05/22/health/hydroxychloroquine-coronavirus-lancet-study/index.html].

CNN: "hydroxychloroquine doesn't work"

Source: [https://www.cnn.com/2020/05/11/health/hydroxychloroquine-doesnt-work-coronavirus/index.html].

CNN: "no benefit, higher death rate"

Source: [https://www.cnn.com/2020/04/21/health/hydroxychloroquine-veterans-study/index.html].

Washington Post

The *Washington Post* has gone as far as quoting a *single* study on the site medrxiv.org that had yet to be peer-reviewed or published. We have seen from the ICL prediction how dangerous non-peer-reviewed articles can be.

Old Saw: Believe It, or Be Mocked

The leftist mainstream media attack and mock any scientist who disagrees with their propagandized agenda. For instance, French epidemiologist Dr. Didier Raoult treated eighty of his COVID-19 patients with hydroxychloroquine and azithromycin. He observed improvements in all of his patients except one advanced case, where the patient was eighty-six years old. How did the mainstream media report this research team's findings? He was attacked as a fraud and mocked.

Source: [https://www.rt.com/op-ed/484102-raoult-chloroquine-coronavirus-treatment/].

Social Media Biased Censorship

YouTube Censors Doctors on Hydroxychloroquine Facts

YouTube called the video dangerous! Later, YouTube reinstated video(s).

Source: [https://sharylattkisson.com/2020/05/youtube-censorship-of-hydroxychloroquine-facts/].

Facebook Censors Information on Hydroxychloroquine

Facebook removed posts reporting on hydroxychloroquine's positive effects, including posts from foreign presidents, such as Brazilian President Jair Bolsonaro.

Source: [https://www.web24.news/u/2020/04/after-twitter-facebook-and-instagram-censor-brazilian-president-jair-bolsonaro.html].

Source: [https://www.thegatewaypundit.com/2020/07/jair-bolsonaro-holds-package-hydroxychloroquine-announces-now-coronavirus-negative/].

Twitter Censors Tweets on Hydroxychloroquine

Twitter deleted tweets from Rudy Giuliani on hydroxychloroquine for violation of rules on coronavirus misinformation.

But 6,200 Doctors Use Hydroxychloroquine to Treat COVID-19

A survey of over 6,200 doctors from thirty countries chooses hydroxychloroquine as the most effective therapy. These international doctors have an overwhelmingly positive response to the use of hydroxychloroquine to treat their COVID-19 patients.

Source: [https://www.sermo.com/press-releases/largest-statistically-significant-study-by-6200-multi-country-physicians-on-covid-19-uncovers-treatment-patterns-and-puts-pandemic-in-context/].

Source: [https://nypost.com/2020/04/02/hydroxychloroquine-most-effective-coronavirus-treatment-poll/].

Dr. Fauci Does *Not* Recommend Doctors Use Hydroxychloroquine

The NIAID and Dr. Fauci recommended against using the drug. The reasoning provided by Dr. Fauci was an increase in sudden cardiac death.

Source: [https://www.npr.org/sections/coronavirus-live-updates/2020/04/21/840341224/nih-panel-recommends-against-drug-combination-trump-has-promoted-for-covid-19].

The American College of Cardiology Disagrees with Dr. Fauci

The American College of Cardiology disagreed with Dr. Fauci. The ACC noted that hydroxychloroquine had been used for the last fifty years to treat malaria, lupus, and rheumatoid arthritis. **"Several hundred million courses of chloroquine have been used worldwide making it one of the most widely used drugs in history, without reports of arrhythmic death under World Health Organization surveillance."**

Source: [https://www.acc.org/latest-in-cardiology/articles/2020/03/27/14/00/ventricular-arrhythmia-risk-due-to-hydroxychloroquine-azithromycin-treatment-for-covid-19].

Peter Navarro Disagrees with Dr. Fauci

Peter Navarro, President Trump's trade adviser, also disagreed with Dr. Fauci regarding hydroxychloroquine. While Navarro isn't an MD, he has a Ph.D. and can read and understand *"statistical studies, whether it's in medicine, the law, economics or whatever."*

I am left to wonder, with such insurmountable evidence for the use of hydroxychloroquine to treat COVID-19, what reason could Dr. Fauci have to discredit the use of hydroxychloroquine and call its use anecdotal?

FDA Revokes Emergency Usage of Hydroxychloroquine

On June 15, 2020, the FDA revoked hydroxychloroquine's emergency usage, as it deemed the drug unlikely to be effective and in light of the adverse cardiac events.

Source: [https://www.fda.gov/news-events/press-announcements/coronavirus-covid-19-update-fda-revokes-emergency-use-authorization-chloroquine-and].

Spain

In Spain, more than 70 percent of medical professionals use hydroxychloroquine to treat COVID-19 patients. This drug was rated "the most effective therapy" by 75 percent of the doctors.

Source: [https://articles.mercola.com/sites/articles/archive/2020/07/15/hydroxychloroquine-for-coronavirus.aspx?cid_source=dnl&cid_medium=email&cid_content=art1HL&cid=20200715Z1&mid=DM593343&rid=916876750].

U.S. Study: Hydroxychloroquine Cuts Mortality in Half

A study of 2,541 COVID-19 patients from the Henry Ford Health Center in Michigan found that untreated patients' mortality rate was 26.4 percent. If given the drug hydroxychloroquine, the mortality rate was cut in half—13.5 percent.

Source: [https://www.ijidonline.com/article/S1201-9712(20)30534-8/fulltext].

Source: [https://www.theepochtimes.com/hydroxychloroquine-lowers-covid-19-death-rate-us-study-finds_3410208.html/amp?__twitter_impression=true].

What Does Cutting the Mortality Rate in Half Mean?

Fatality rates and mortality rates are used to explain the death rate of COVID-19, but they are not interchangeable rates. This difference can be illustrated with a sample population of 100 people. Imagine twenty people became infected, and one of the infected people died. The proportion of people who died after infection, the fatality rate, would be 5 percent. However, since only 1 percent of the population died, the mortality rate is 1 percent.

$$\text{Case Fatality Rate} = \frac{\text{\# of Deaths}}{\text{\# of Infections}} = \frac{1}{20} = 0.05 \times 100 = 5\%$$

$$\text{Mortality Rate} = \frac{\text{\# of Deaths}}{\text{\# of Population}} = \frac{1}{100} = 0.01 \times 100 = 1\%$$

Source: [https://newslit.org/updates/case-fatality-rate-vs-mortality-rate/].

CNN Reverses Itself on Hydroxychloroquine

July 3, 2020. Source: [https://www.cnn.com/2020/07/02/health/hydroxychloroquine-coronavirus-detroit-study/index.html].

Surgisphere Faked Anti-hydroxychloroquine Study

A Surgisphere report stated that it had gathered data from hundreds of hospitals worldwide detailing hydroxychloroquine's harmful effects. This study was published in both the *Lancet* and *NEJM*.

Dr. Fauci and WHO used this discredited study to broadcast to the world that hydroxychloroquine is not effective. The study was used as a reason by the CDC and WHO to immediately halt hydroxychloroquine studies, which it did here and around the globe.

The fake news media widely reported this story with relish, as it fits their anti-Trump anti-hydroxychloroquine narrative.

The study was retracted by both publications for vast inaccuracies, but not before the paper had done its damage, maligning the drug hydroxychloroquine and halting research.

As usual, the fake news media barely mentioned the study's retraction.

This raises the question; how did this study get past strict peer-review procedures to be accepted by the two most trusted medical journals? Why did Surgisphere create this false study? Was Surgisphere paid for this study? Something stinks pretty bad here.

I should also point out that neither the *Lancet* nor the *NEJM* detected the vast inaccuracies in their peer-review process. It was open letters sent to the *Lancet* from hundreds of researchers questioning Surgisphere's data sets' validity that uncovered the fake data that led to the retractions.

The Surgisphere data sets included fake data and information cited from some of the hardest-hit hospitals in New York, New Jersey, and Illinois. However, when contacted, these hospitals told researchers they never contributed data to the Surgisphere study.

Source: [https://www.the-scientist.com/news-opinion/concerns-build-about-surgisphere-corporations-dataset-67605].

That was just the tip of the spear, as more and more data discrepancies began to show up and accumulate.

Source: [https://www.the-scientist.com/news-opinion/lancet-retracts-surgispheres-study-on-hydroxychloroquine-67613].

Source:
[https://articles.mercola.com/sites/articles/archive/2020/07/08/the-lancet-retraction-hydroxychloroquine-clinical-trial.aspx].

The Surgisphere website has been taken down and its Twitter account deleted.

America's Frontline Doctors

I have never seen the level of orchestrated censorship directed against America's Frontline Doctors' videos and website. This brave group of "frontline" doctors details the damaging misinformation propagandized about hydroxychloroquine by the fake mainstream media news. Misinformation that, in their opinion, is costing many Americans their lives.

Within hours, the group's live stream gathered 17 million views before Facebook censored it. Its videos on YouTube and Twitter were also censored, following Facebook, and labeled "misinformation." Its website AmericasFrontlineDoctors.com went dark and was removed by Squarespace a few hours after their live feed. Squarespace stated that America's Frontline Doctors' website violated their terms of agreement.

Numerous developers offered a censorship-free hosting for the website. America's Frontline Doctors now have a new URL and website: [https://americasfrontlinedoctorsummit.com/].

Dr. Simone Gold is an emergency care physician based in Los Angeles. The video of America's Frontline Doctors' press conference at the front of the U.S. Supreme Court can be viewed here:

[https://www.bitchute.com/video/zro4GsUupOwk/].

America's Frontline Doctors also produced two longer three-hour videos, six hours in total. These videos feature numerous doctors taking the podium to explain their knowledge and positive experiences with hydroxychloroquine. These videos are as much for other doctors and medical support staff as they are for the general population.

These videos were censored and deleted from every social media platform.

Remember, these are medical doctors providing their medical opinions based on their experience treating patients with COVID-19. Who are Google, Facebook, and Twitter to censor these doctors? Again, this illustrating the high level of corruption and censorship being implemented on these leftist social media platforms.

America's Frontline Doctors group is correcting misinformation being promoted about hydroxychloroquine. I recommend seeing a few of their shorter, also censored videos.

So important are these videos that Donald Trump, Jr., retweeted the video; the video was deleted, and his Twitter account was restricted for twelve hours.

President Trump retweeted the video. While his account was not affected, Twitter did delete the video.

However, you can visit the censorship-free substitute for YouTube called LBRY, search for "American Frontline Doctors" to see the censored videos. Judge for yourself if these doctors are credible or not.

But Wait, There's More!

Imagine a country that embraced the use of hydroxychloroquine. How would that country have fared against COVID-19? We don't have to imagine because many countries use hydroxychloroquine regularly for malaria.

The COVID-19 death rate in these countries listed below that use hydroxychloroquine is about one-hundredth (1/100) of countries that do not use hydroxychloroquine (data date July 31, 2020).

Country	Population	Cases	Deaths
Uganda	45M	1,176	4
Ethiopia	115M	17,502	274
Nigeria	21M	43,151	879
Pakistan	197M	278,000	5,971
India	1.4B	1.7M	38,830

You can compare this data with countries that do not use hydroxychloroquine and draw your own conclusions from the data. The data clearly shows hydroxychloroquine is not only an effective treatment but a prophylactic as well.

One More Hydroxychloroquine (HCQ) Study

This is the most extensive multi-country study I have ever seen. There are 1.8 billion people in the HCQ treatment group and 663 million people in the control group. The treatment group has a 77.4% lower death rate.

Source: [https://hcqtrial.com/].

Corruption in Our Medical Community and Government is Frightening

With data from scientific studies, countries using hydroxychloroquine, and brave physicians like America's Frontline Doctors, you have the FDA stopping the emergency use of hydroxychloroquine for treating COVID-19. You have doctors being threatened by medical licensing boards with the loss of medical licenses for prescribing hydroxychloroquine to save their patients' lives. Governors are threatening pharmacists, who are being told not to fulfill prescriptions by doctors for hydroxychloroquine with a threat of losing their pharmacy license.

At what point did it become permissible for a state governor and politicians to step in between a doctor and patient to supersede a doctor's medical judgment to prevent medical treatment? The corruption in the medical community and our government is frightening.

Source: [https://www.youtube.com/watch?v=wr8CpMudkrE].

Source: [https://www.thegatewaypundit.com/2020/04/doctors-threatened-13000-fine-prescribing-hydroxychloroquine-coronavirus-treatment/].

I believe, at the most conservative level, our scientific studies that show hydroxychloroquine treatment cuts mortality in half. Whether you believe the COVID-19 death count is 130,000 or 50,000, hydroxychloroquine can cut the mortality rate in half and would appear to me to have prevented thousands of these deaths.

How Many Thousands of Deaths Did the Fake News Media Cause?

How many COVID-19 patients and their doctors were frightened of using hydroxychloroquine because of the fake news media reports? How many of those patients died who may have lived? Don't expect the fake news media, social media platforms, or state governors who restricted access to hydroxychloroquine to accept any responsibility or be held accountable for the unnecessary COVID-19 deaths they caused. The fake news, social media platforms, and Democrats have each other's back.

Profit Before Patients?

A COVID-19 vaccine can make millions, if not billions, of dollars for the pharmaceutical companies.

It has been mentioned many times that the controversy regarding hydroxychloroquine is based on wanting a vaccine cure instead of a treatment. Does this have any validity? Again, I am not a detective or investigative reporter. I can say some comprehensive studies against hydroxychloroquine have come under fire for being inaccurate, such as the Surgisphere study.

Chapter 13: Scamdemic Continues.

Real pandemics don't rely on faulty prediction models, biased reporting, politicized science, and inflated death statistics.

Source: [https://www.cdc.gov/nchs/nvss/vsrr/covid_weekly/index.htm].

Some Democrat states, like New York, remain in a partial lockdown. The fake news media and Democrats are projecting a second wave and more lockdowns. That's interesting since the first wave never occurred. Again, in my opinion, these lockdowns have nothing to do with science and are politically motivated.

As of July 4, 2020, the Country's COVID-19 Deaths Still Staying Flatlined – No Second Wave

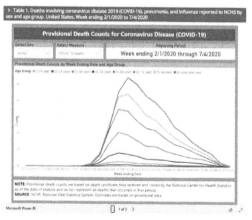

Source: [https://www.cdc.gov/nchs/nvss/vsrr/covid_weekly/index.htm].

The U.S. Annual Death by Disease, the book cover graphic, is dated March 30, 2020. It shows the number of COVID-19 deaths at the time of the lockdowns.

I have updated this chart as of June 20, 2020, using this provisional inflated death number for COVID-19. Compared to other annual deaths in the United States from 2019, COVID-19 deaths are still not a significant cause of death even with the inflated COVID-19 death tolls. COVID-19 deaths plotted in the chart are provisional COVID-19 deaths minus influenza deaths.

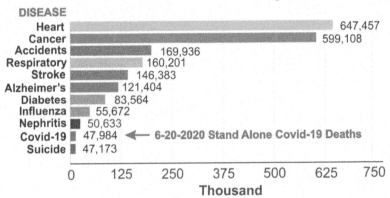

U.S. Annual Death By Disease

DISEASE

Disease	Deaths
Heart	647,457
Cancer	599,108
Accidents	169,936
Respiratory	160,201
Stroke	146,383
Alzheimer's	121,404
Diabetes	83,564
Influenza	55,672
Nephritis	50,633
Covid-19	47,984 ⟵ 6-20-2020 Stand Alone Covid-19 Deaths
Suicide	47,173

0   125   250   375   500   625   750

Thousand

REF: https://www.cdc.gov/nchs/fastats/leading-causes-of-death.htm

I have provided information ignored or distorted by the fake news media. The country is now struggling to reopen, while Democrat governors are doing everything they can to delay reopening their states and are threatening a new lockdown to prevent a "second wave" of COVID-19, which, as noted before, is interesting since the first wave never occurred.

Hospitalizations stay times for COVID-19 patients are down 50 percent.

Twenty percent to 30 percent of hospitalizations for nonrelated COVID-19 reasons are reclassified as COVID-19 because of a positive COVID-19 test. Remember the incentive programs for hospitals.

Models Have Failed Repeatably Since March 2020 – So Democrats Use the Models to Keep Schools Closed

Does this make any sense?

The American Academy of Pediatrics and the Hospital for Sick Children in Toronto is recommending all students return to school with no restrictions, meaning no face masks and no social distancing. Children have zero risks from COVID-19 and rarely transmit the disease.

Regarding the teaching staff, —50 percent of teachers from kindergarten through twelfth grade are under forty-one years of age. Eighty percent are under fifty-five years of age. These are low-risk populations. For older teachers, it is recommended to take proper precautions or work from home.

Source: Dr. Scott Atlas, Hoover Institute – Tucker Carlson interview Fox News (undated).

According to America's Frontline Doctors, there is not one documented case of a child passing COVID-19 to a teacher.

According to the CDC as of July 25, 2020:

Date	Start	End	State	Sex	Age g.	COVI...	Total..	Pneu..	Pneu..	Influ..	Pneu..	Foo
07/29/2020	02/01/2020	07/25/2020	United St..	All	Under 1 y..	14	8,459	77	2	14	103	
07/29/2020	02/01/2020	07/25/2020	United St..	All	1-4 years	9	1,620	54	2	41	102	
07/29/2020	02/01/2020	07/25/2020	United St..	All	5-14 years	19	2,498	84	6	50	147	
					Total	42			Total	105		

Source: [https://data.cdc.gov/NCHS/Provisional-COVID-19-Death-Counts-by-Sex-Age-and-S/9bhg-hcku].

Between the dates of February 1, 2020, and July 25, 2020, for children under fifteen years old, there were 105 influenzas deaths and only forty-two COVID-19 deaths. And please keep in mind the generous inflatable CDC guidelines for reporting COVID-19 deaths.

We don't close our schools for influenza, which is twice as deadly as COVID-19 for children.

Back to Sweden

Sweden kept its schools open without suffering any additional adverse effects to its children, as compared to countries that did lockdown. For children up to nineteen, Sweden's infection rate among children is 0.05 percent. In Finland, where they did shut down, the infection rate for children up to nineteen years old is also 0.05 percent.

Source: [https://www.reuters.com/article/us-health-coronavirus-sweden-schools-idUSKCN24G2IS].

Children Are Not a Vector for Spreading COVID-19

According to a German study of 2,045 children from thirteen schools, children in schools are not a vector for infecting teachers with COVID-19.

"It is rather the opposite," Professor Berner told a press conference. "Children act more as a brake on infection. Not every infection that reaches them is passed on."

Source: [https://news.yahoo.com/german-study-finds-no-evidence-164704005.html].

CDC Recommends Opening Schools in Fall

Source: [https://www.cdc.gov/coronavirus/2019-ncov/community/schools-childcare/reopening-schools.html].

Not Following "the Science" *Fur Ihre Sicherheit*

Still, despite the science, state governors are keeping schools closed. We can also blame the teachers' unions petitioning for school closures. Remember their propaganda motto, **Fur Ihre Sicherheit** (translation: *For Your Safety)*.

Teacher's union official who lobbies to keep schools closed, vacations in Puerto Rico where the CDC stated to avoid travel. More liberal hypocrisy. Source: [https://www.bizpacreview.com/2021/01/02/teachers-union-exec-lobbied-for-classroom-boycotts-over-covid-shares-posh-vacay-pics-from-puerto-rico-1011795/]

Fake News Still Propagating Fear Over Facts

The fake news is relentless in its fearmongering propaganda. The latest phony news blitz is the continued criticism of Florida for easing its lockdown on residents. A FOX 35 investigation revealed that the increase in COVID-19 cases was inflated by misreporting test results from laboratories.

Source: [https://www.breitbart.com/local/2020/07/14/fox-35-investigation-reveals-inflated-florida-covid-19-numbers/?utm_source=newsletter&utm_medium=email&utm_term=daily&utm_campaign=20200714].

More Florida Counting Troubles

I am sticking with Florida because this is the focus of the fake news media. Interestingly some labs in Florida are reporting 100 percent of tests as positive. It turns out that many labs are reporting only positive test results. Reporting only positive results makes the percentage of positive tests look higher than they are.

It is *not* accepted that each positive test result should be counted as a case. Yet the fake news media does just that—one positive test equals one case. Just testing positive doesn't make you sick. To be correctly counted as a case, you need to be ill and test positive. Just another way the fake news media inflates the "case" numbers.

Another problem is when an individual has multiple tests at different labs. A single person testing positive can be counted three or four times by other labs.

Source: [https://articles.mercola.com/sites/articles/archive/2020/07/27/coronavirus-infection-rate-in-usa.aspx?cid_source=dnl&cid_medium=email&cid_content=art1HL&cid=20200727Z1&mid=DM607311&rid=926057347].

Common Cold Antibodies Can Trigger False Positive Test

The common cold is a coronavirus. Therefore, it can also trigger a false positive test for COVID-19. So how useful are these tests, and what do they measure—how many people in the U.S. had colds?

How to get an antibody test

Decisions about testing are made by state or local ☑ health departments or healthcare providers.

Antibody tests for COVID-19 are available through healthcare providers and laboratories. Check with your healthcare provider to see if they offer antibody tests and whether you should get one.

Guidance on Interpreting COVID-19 Test Results 🔬 ☑ : A guide for understanding test results and determining what actions to take.

What do your results mean?

If you test positive

- A positive test result shows you may have antibodies from an infection with the virus that causes COVID-19. However, there is a chance a positive result means that you have antibodies from an infection with a virus from the same family of viruses (called coronaviruses), such as the one that causes the common cold.

Source: [https://www.cdc.gov/coronavirus/2019-ncov/testing/serology-overview.html].

Cases vs. Deaths

As the lockdowns eased and people mingled, an increase in COVID-19 cases would be expected. The fake news media will perform their usual handwringing over the rise in positive tests, spinning the increase in COVID-19 tests as a failure. It is not. Here's why.

The fake news mainstream media is not telling you is that the increase in COVID-19 positive tests does not result in more deaths. In addition, the increase in cases is not necessarily alarming. Why? Because the rise in COVID-19 cases is with young, healthy people. These healthy people are our low-risk population.

Once the low-risk population has been infected, they are immune. When you are immune, you are no longer a carrier for the disease. When enough of the population becomes immune, the disease doesn't have the carriers to infect the still-vulnerable people. They call this herd immunity.

Pay attention to the deaths and listen to what the real unbiased scientists say, like Dr. Michael Levitt, Dr. John Ioannidis, Anders Tegnell, and Dr. Jennifer Lighter. These battle-harden scientists have proven themselves to tell the truth despite the fake news media.

Fake News Reports Hospitals are Overrun

Nurses are dancing as their hospital is supposedly overrun with COVID-19 patients.

Source: [https://www.prophecyportal.org/2020/12/26/nurses-dance-in-cringeworthy-tiktok-video-at-a-time-when-hospitals-are-supposedly-overrun-due-to-covid/]

Empty hospitals.

Source: [https://www.prophecyportal.org/2020/12/22/virtually-empty-d-c-area-hospital-captured-on-video-as-government-media-perpetuate-covid-surge-myths/]

Next Sham Coming Up – Mandatory Testing and Vaccination

If you believe mandatory face masks are an inconvenience to be allowed to enter public stores and buildings, wait until you see the mandatory testing and vaccination scheme the Democrats are hatching. It would make George Orwell proud. Historically didn't we see this done in Nazi Germany?

Source: [https://www.washingtontimes.com/news/2020/apr/8/anthony-fauci-sets-stage-mandatory-vaccine/].

Source: [https://www.timesunion.com/news/article/Protest-against-mandatory-COVID-19-vaccines-15330967.php].

PCR COVID-19 Tests are Completely Unreliable

The PCR tests are another farce. In NY, they are continually broadcasting Public Service Announcements (PSA) to get tested for COVID-19 even if you're not sick. Why? PCR testing is not accurate. The tests appear to be designed to provide a high number of "false" positives results. Why do I say this? Here's why. The tests are so insensitive that they need to amplify the genetic snippets they are looking for to be detected. Each round of amplification is called a cycle. After 35 cycles of amplification, scientists say the test is unreliable. However, the World Health Organization recommends tests set to 45 cycles. What? For greater detail, read the source article.

Source: [https://articles.mercola.com/sites/articles/archive/2020/11/19/covid-testing-fraud-fuels-casedemic.aspx].

Elon Musk

Elon Musk, one of our country's smartest men, got tested four times in one day. Using the same test, same equipment, and same nurse, two tests came back positive, and two tests came back negative. On Nov. 13, he wrote on his Twitter feed.

"Something extremely bogus is going on. Was tested for covid four times today. Two tests came back negative, two came back positive. Same machine, same test, same nurse. Rapid antigen test from BD."

Source: [https://nypost.com/2020/11/13/elon-musk-continues-to-cast-doubt-about-covid-19-test-results/].

I agree. You can't sustain a Scamdemic with a panic population without creating fear. This fear allows the government to keep the population under control and obedient.

The New Nazi Tattoo - Quantum Dot Technology

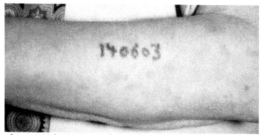

Auschwitz Survivor - Air Force photo by Rudy Purificato / Public Domain

Advances in tracking and vaccine compliance have surpassed the old Nazi methods of tattoo identification. Today we have "Quantum Dot" technology. A quantum dot is an invisible microscopic tattoo developed by MIT that records your vaccine history in your skin. The tattoo is made up of a pattern of tiny "quantum dots" that can be read with an infrared smartphone device.

This technology was developed with funding from the Bill and Melinda Gates Foundation

Source: [https://21stcenturywire.com/2019/12/23/bill-gates-develops-new-id-tattoo-to-check-for-vaccinations/].

Next Up - H.R. 6666 — COVID-19 Testing, Reaching and Contacting Everyone (TRACE) Act

Here is where the Quantum Dot tattoo technology gains traction. If you needed any more proof the leftist socialist Democrats hate America and our constitutional freedom, this is it.

Sponsored by Representative Bobby L. Rush, a Democrat in Illinois, the bill was introduced May 1, 2020, and co-sponsored by sixty-four Democrats.

The bill, if passed, allocates $100 billion to test and monitor every citizen for COVID-19. This bill infringes and breaches many of our constitutional rights. That fact hasn't stopped Democrat support.

For instance, if you test positive, you could be ordered into quarantine (home or government facility) and have your children removed from your care.

Source: [https://articles.mercola.com/sites/articles/archive/2020/06/02/hr-6666-covid-19-government-surveillance.aspx].

If passed, I'm sure the bill will incorporate Quantum Dot tattoos to ensure mandatory vaccine compliance.

Can you imagine a future where you must have your arm scanned for your "Quantum Tattoo" to be allowed to enter a school, store, public building, or facility? Isn't this precisely the foundation the Democrats are trying to build into the law with the H.R. 6666 COVID-19 testing? Remember *Fur Ihre Sicherheit!*

Following is a chart showing the number of cases (green) and COVID-19 deaths (red). The CDC states that only 6% of the reported COVID-19 deaths (in RED) are from COVID-19 alone. The rest are comorbidities, like a fatal gunshot wound to the head, being reported as a COVID-19 death because of a positive COVID-19 test.

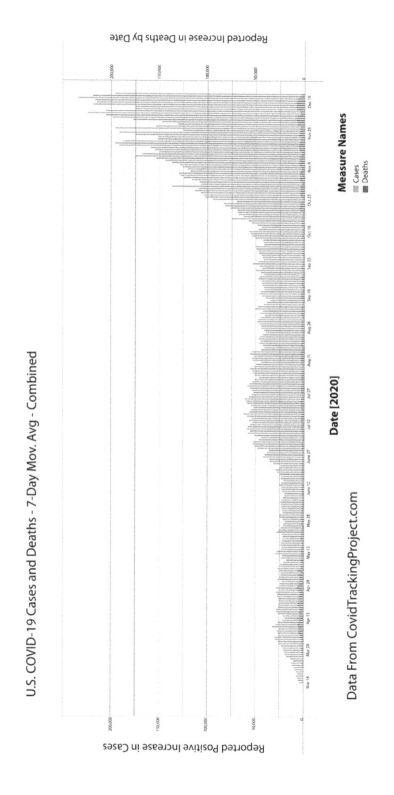

U.S. COVID-19 Cases and Deaths - 7-Day Mov. Avg - Combined

Reported Positive Increase in Cases

Reported Increase in Deaths by Date

Date [2020]

Data From CovidTrackingProject.com

Measure Names
Cases
Deaths

155

John Hopkins Reports –
Relatively No Additional Deaths in 2020 Due to COVID-19

On Nov. 22, 2020, John Hopkins published this truthful report. It created such a "liberal" furor that John Hopkins had to delete the report from its website. Another example of "Cancel Culture" intimidation and fact censoring.

From the original John Hopkins report:

> *Surprisingly, the deaths of older people stayed the same before and after COVID-19. Since COVID-19 mainly affects the elderly, experts expected an increase in the percentage of deaths in older age groups. However, this increase is not seen from the CDC data. In fact, the percentages of deaths among all age groups remain relatively the same.*

Transfer of Deaths

If you look at the death toll numbers for other causes of death, they all decreased in proportion to the deaths reported for COVID-19

From the original John Hopkins report:

> *This trend is completely contrary to the pattern observed in all previous years. Interestingly, as depicted in the table below, the total decrease in deaths by other causes almost exactly equals the increase in deaths by COVID-19. This suggests, according to Briand, that the COVID-19 death toll is misleading. Briand believes that deaths due to heart diseases, respiratory diseases, influenza, and pneumonia may instead be recategorized as being due to COVID-19.*

Source: [https://www.thegatewaypundit.com/2020/11/johns-hopkins-study-mysteriously-disappears-shows-spite-covid-no-deaths-2020-prior-years].

Source: [https://pjmedia.com/news-and-politics/matt-margolis/2020/11/27/johns-hopkins-study-saying-covid-19-has-relatively-no-effect-on-deaths-in-u-s-deleted-after-publication-n1178930].

Wayback Machine Link to Original Study Source:
[https://web.archive.org/web/20201126223119/https://www.jhunewslett
er.com/article/2020/11/a-closer-look-at-u-s-deaths-due-to-covid-19].

If there aren't over 300,000 excessive deaths in the US, as according to
the report, there can't be an excess of 300,000 deaths due to COVID-19 as
the liberal legacy media and their brainwashed zombie followers
continually repeat.

Support Against the Scamdemic is Growing

Top Canadian Scientists Tells Government the Coronavirus is "The Greatest Hoax Ever Perpetrated on an Unsuspecting Public"

Source: [https://www.thegatewaypundit.com/2020/11/top-canadian-
pathologist-tells-alberta-government-covid-greatest-hoax-ever-
perpetrated-unsuspecting-public/].

Rand Paul stated the new lockdowns, "They're completely arbitrary."

Source: [https://www.theepochtimes.com/rand-paul-new-coronavirus-
lockdowns-are-completely-arbitrary_3586096.html].

Rep. Jim Jordan Says Some COVID-19 Restrictions Have 'Gotten So Ridiculous'

Source: [https://www.theepochtimes.com/rep-jim-jordan-says-some-
covid-19-restrictions-have-gotten-so-ridiculous_3590081.html].

Studies Prove Lockdowns Don't Control COVID-19

Source: [https://www.aier.org/article/lockdowns-do-not-control-the-
coronavirus-the-evidence/].

The legacy and social media are still censoring any opposition information
that the China Virus isn't a pandemic because they still need a pandemic

to force American citizens into compliance, attack President Trump, and rig the 2020 Presidential election

Beginning in 2021, Twitter will remove any tweets it considers misinformation about vaccines or that COVID-19 (the China Virus) is not real or dangerous. I guess this book information will be censored off Twitter as well as Facebook.

Democrats Want Continued Totalitarian Lockdowns Even After Vaccine.

President Trump has delivered on his promise to provide a vaccine for the China Virus within one year. As of mid-December 2020, over two million doses of the vaccine are being distributed across the country. To prove how democrats want to continue the totalitarian lockdown, they are floating talking heads on major news networks promoting continued lockdowns. NBC's Dr. Vin Gupta stated that people should restrict travel and continue to wear masks after being vaccinated.

Senator Ted Cruz (R-TX) responded on Twitter, "This is a bizarre, lunatic, totalitarian cult. It's not about vaccines or protecting people's lives — it is instead profoundly anti-science and is only focused on absolute govt control of every aspect of our lives."

Source: [https://www.dailywire.com/news/nbc-doctor-masks-necessary-travel-restricted-even-after-vaccine?utm_campaign].

Dec. 19, 2020 Deaths from Gunshot Wounds Still Reported as COVID-19 Deaths

You may have thought this a joke when you first read that a gunshot wound to the head was reported as COVID-19 death. It was not, and it is still occurring across the country in every coroner's office. The government's mandate to inflate COVID-19 deaths force coroners to classify death by gunshot as COVID-19 if the person has a positive test for COVID-19. Why would a coroner perform a COVID-19 test on a corpse? I think it's a financial incentive? Remember the COVID-19 tests and death chart. Anyone who tested positive, even false positive as we saw with Elon Musk, will have their death classified as COVID-19, regardless of cause.

This has been happening since the beginning of the COVID-19 scamdemic.

Here is a December 2020 video from a Grand County Coroner:

[https://www.air.tv/watch?v=lDm_pwxBQZyU5IRDf3eZKA].

Source: [https://www.bizpacreview.com/2020/12/18/colorado-coroner-expresses-shock-over-inflated-covid-death-tallies-including-bodies-with-gunshots-1007116].

More Clinical Studies That Prove Wearing Facemasks Are Ineffective Nonsense.

The Association of American Physicians and Surgeons Clinical study conclusion: Wearing masks (other than N95) will not be effective at preventing SARS-CoV-2 transmission, whether worn as source control or as PPE.

Source: [https://aapsonline.org/mask-facts/].

Source: [https://www.nejm.org/doi/full/10.1056/NEJMp2006372?af=R&rss=currentIssue].

Source: [https://pubmed.ncbi.nlm.nih.gov/32203710/].

I can't keep track of how many times the CDC has flip-flopped on the facemask issue. The CDC may flip-flop, but the science remains constant. Below is a CDC study dated 9-11-2020.

CDC STUDY: 85% of COVID-19 patients report 'always' or 'often' wearing a mask – In Other Words, Masks Don't Work

TABLE. Characteristics of symptomatic adults ≥18 years who were outpatients in 11 academic health care facilities and who received positive and negative SARS-CoV-2 test results (N = 314)* — United States, July 1–29, 2020

Characteristic	No. (%)		
	Case-patients (n = 154)	Control participants (n = 160)	P-value
Reported use of cloth face covering or mask 14 days before illness onset (missing = 2)			
Never	6 (3.9)	5 (3.1)	0.86
Rarely	6 (3.9)	6 (3.8)	
Sometimes	11 (7.2)	7 (4.4)	
Often	22 (14.4)	23 (14.5)	
Always	108 (70.6)	118 (74.2)	

Source: [https://www.cdc.gov/mmwr/volumes/69/wr/mm6936a5.htm].

160

Facemasks Cause More Problems Than They Solve.

Quote: There is no good evidence that facemasks protect the public against infection with respiratory viruses, including COVID-19. 6

Source: [https://www.ncbi.nlm.nih.gov/pmc/articles/PMC7323223/].

In my opinion, the government forcing you to wear a facemask is its training program in population control, compliance, and obedience - Facemasks are initiated without public consent or scientific validity.

Did You Hear the Latest?

I'm beginning to hear the drumbeat of a mutated or variant form of the COVID-19 virus. Wow, just in time to re-create another virus Scamdemic to keep everyone locked down now that we have a vaccine for the original COVID-19 China Virus.

Chapter 14 - Stealing The 2020 Presidential Election

When Joe Biden stated that his campaign had created the, "most extensive and inclusive voter fraud organization in the history of American politics"

I believe him.

Source: [https://www.breitbart.com/politics/2020/10/24/joe-biden-touts-most-extensive-inclusive-voter-fraud-organization-in-history-of-american-politics/].

Pre-election shenanigans

The Democrat's pre-election shenanigans began with using the China Virus (COVID-19).

The China Virus and Mail-In Ballots

As I predicted, in the first edition, the China Virus "pandemic" was the means to the end to weaponize mail-in ballots to steal the 2020 presidential election. Despite what the liberal democrats are saying today regarding the safety of mail-in voting, in the past, liberals warned us that mail-in voting is a way to commit massive fraud.

New York Times article 2010:

[https://www.nytimes.com/2012/10/07/us/politics/as-more-vote-by-mail-faulty-ballots-could-impact-elections.html].

Jimmy Carter led a study in 2005 that determined the potential for massive fraud via mail-in voting.

[https://justthenews.com/politics-policy/elections/long-trump-bipartisan-group-elder-statesmen-flagged-mail-ballot-fraud].

Recent examples of voter fraud.

[https://justthenews.com/politics-policy/elections/yes-america-there-voter-fraud-these-recent-cases-prove-it].

Democrats used the China Virus pandemic to pass state laws to make mail-in voting cheating much more effortless.

[https://townhall.com/tipsheet/katiepavlich/2020/12/07/mark-levin-details-how-democrats-changed-the-rules-on-fraud-n2581151].

[https://www.newsmax.com/politics/democrats-mcdaniel-voter-fraud-pennsylvania/2020/11/05/id/995571/].

Depending upon the State, Democrats weaponized mail-voting for fraud by removing the standard safeguards. They petition the courts to remove the need for a ballot signature, no signature verification, no postmark date, and extended dates to receive mail-in ballots. In other words, everything that controlled the process needed for fair elections.

I'm not a lawyer, but in reading about these changes and the subsequent lawsuits, I understand that to change voter laws legally, the changes must go through the legislative branch. In some states, the changes must be put on the ballot for people to vote to accept these changes. The Democrats didn't have time to change the laws legally. They had an election to rig and only a few months to do it in. So the mail-in voter rule changes were put through by the executive branch using the courts. When the Democrats changed the voting laws in this manner, they violated their state and our federal Constitution. Put aside the fact for the moment; the Democrats used these mail-in voter law changes to institute massive voter and election fraud; it is because of the violation of their state and our federal Constitution that these mail-in votes are being challenged and contested in the courts.

President Donald Trump warned of massive mail-in voter fraud, and he was correct.

Unfortunately, each voter and election fraud case being brought before the courts are currently being dismissed before any evidence is presented. It appears our judges and courts are saying the Trump campaign doesn't have the proper standing to bring the cases forward. This question of standing is something I do not understand. Wouldn't the greater justice be served by investigating the criminal behavior of election and voter fraud?

Chris Krebs – The Most Secure Election in US History?

Many liberals point to fired Director of Cyber Security Chris Krebs, who stated that the 2020 election was the most secure in US history. However, during the US Senate Homeland Security Committee on 12-18-2020, he testified to two things,

1) Some Dominion voting machines were connected to the Internet.

2) When he said the election was the most secure, he was only referring to foreign country election interference via the Internet. He was not referring to any other fraud, such as mail-in voting fraud. This was before we learned of the Cyber Attacks on our government agencies under his watch.

But, to listen to liberals, they used what he said as a blanket statement to express that every aspect of the election was secure, and this is not true.

Twenty Federal Agencies Under Cyber Attack under Chris Krebs Watch

A few weeks later, we discovered that under Chris Krebs's watch, no less than twenty major government agencies have been under cyber-attacks from foreign actors, including China, Iran, and Russia that began in March 2020.

Source: [https://us-cert.cisa.gov/ncas/alerts/aa20-352a].

Chris Krebs accepts responsibility for missing the cyber-attacks on our country.

[https://www.washingtonexaminer.com/news/cybersecurity-expert-chris-krebs-accepts-responsibility-massive-hack-russia].

So it stands to reason he also missed every incident of election fraud too.

John Ratcliffe DNI

John Ratcliffe, the Director of National Intelligence (DNI), had to delay his Dec 18 report accessing the foreign threats to the 2020 election. Even though the report is delayed, John Ratcliffe has confirmed foreign interference in the presidential elections from China, Iran, and Russia. Foreign interference with this election will allow President Trump to invoke emergency powers. This information conflicts with Chris Krebs's statements and could be a contributing factor in President Trump firing him. John Ratcliffe leads 17 intelligence agencies.

Source: [https://www.theepochtimes.com/dni-says-intelligence-will-not-meet-trumps-dec-18-deadline-to-report-foreign-threats-during-election_3621908.html].

The China Delay

The DNI report's delay appears to hinge on two "deep state" intelligence agencies that do not want to release their "damming" information regarding China's influence on the 2020 Presidential Election. Again, in direct contrast to what Chris Krebs stated to congress.

You would think these pre-election shenanigans would be enough. No, not by a long shot.

Legacy and Social Media Censorship

I've written on the Legacy and Social Media censorship. But in light of the presidential election, it is starting to come together with the misinformation and censorship regarding the China Virus. It is evident to me how the legacy media, social media, and Democrats work with one another against the country's best interests.

Twitter, Facebook, and YouTube Censorship

Sidney Powell has had her Twitter account suspended because she linked an article with derogatory information on the Dominion voting machines. She is not the only one. Twitter accounts of **Rudy Giuliani** and Attorney **Lin Wood** have been 'search banned' by Twitter for their posts on voter fraud. Facebook has increased its conservative censorship to include every mention of election and voter fraud with a "fact check" and "dispute" warning.

The mathematician **Bobby Piton** who testified to the Arizona State Legislature about his investigation regarding voter fraud allegations, had his Twitter account suspended after testifying.

According to MRC, Trump's Twitter account has been censored 543 times. Biden's Twitter account, 0 times.

Source: [https://www.newsbusters.org/blogs/techwatch/heather-moon/2020/12/21/twitter-censors-trump-and-campaign-543-times-never-biden].

YouTube removes videos showing election fraud as "misinformation."

Source: [https://nypost.com/2020/12/09/youtube-bans-videos-claiming-2020-presidential-election-fraud/].

YouTube Removes Trump Lawyer's Opening Statement from Senate Committee Hearing

Source: [https://www.theepochtimes.com/youtube-removes-trump-lawyers-opening-statement-from-senate-committee-

hearing_3626087.html?utm_source=news&utm_medium=email&utm_c
ampaign=breaking-2020-12-20-3].

The cancel culture of pretending there isn't any evidence, censoring the evidence that's presented, and labeling any posted information "disputed" or "fact-checked" isn't going to work in a court of law. And that's where this election fraud will eventually be played out.

The Biden Criminal Investigation Cover Up

Any negative information regarding Joe Biden or his son Hunter Biden was censored from the news and shadow banned on social media (if allowed to be posted at all). Six months before the election, the fake news media called Rudy Giuliani, a Russian spy, for disclosing evidence he had on Biden family crimes.

For months leading up to the presidential election, the legacy media and social media claimed that any news of Hunter Biden's corruption was nothing more than right-wing "conspiracy theories" and Russian propaganda/interference to affect our presidential election. Talking heads from every main media outlet claimed they "debunked" the story and ignored the Hunter Biden corruption because they don't report false news. Twitter deleted NY. Post's account for publishing an Oct 14, 2020 article on Hunter Biden's laptop and corruption. The NY Post is the fourth-largest newspaper in the U.S. During the debates, Joe Biden lied to every American that information about his son Hunter Biden's laptop was Russian misinformation. A month after the election, we learn the US Attorney's Office in Delaware has Hunter Biden under criminal investigation for many crimes, including tax evasion and money laundering. Hunter Biden had ties to China, Russia, and Ukraine.

Source: [https://www.theepochtimes.com/gop-senators-hunter-biden-
had-even-more-ties-to-china-kremlin_3585016.html].

The social media suppression worked, according to a Newsweek article.

Source: [https://www.newsweek.com/facebooks-effort-suppress-hunter-
biden-ny-post-story-gave-it-half-reach-major-anti-trump-scoops-
1539954].

The suppression of this information gave Joe Biden an additional 10% more votes in key states.

After the election, the Associated Press reported federal prosecutors subpoenaed Hunter Biden for his business records for more than two dozen entities, including Ukrainian energy firm Burisma and other companies based in China.

50 Former Heads of Security say Hunter Biden Info Russian Disinformation.

During the debates, Joe Bidden told America that he had a letter signed by 50 former heads of security, including James Clapper, Leon Panetta, John Brennan, that the information regarding Hunter Biden is nothing more than Russian disinformation.

Has the legacy media held Joe Biden or any of the former heads of security accountable? No, they did not. The legacy media only hold conservatives and Republicans responsible for their actions.

DOJ and the FBI

When President Trump asked his DOJ and FBI to investigate Hunter Biden, the DOJ Attorney General Barr already knew there were investigations into Hunter Biden. But he kept this information from the President of the United States and the public.

Later we learned that both the FBI and DOJ's Attorney General William Barr knew about Hunter Biden's laptop and criminal investigation long before it became public knowledge. In the FBI case, they had been sitting on the evidence in Biden's laptop for over a year. However, during the debate, when President Trump brought up questions regarding foreign money paid to Hunter Biden, Joe Biden lied to the American people.

AG William Barr knew Joe Biden lied to the American people. Did he come forward with the information about criminal investigations into Hunter Biden? No, he did not. He let President Trump be savaged and lied about in the legacy and social media, accused of spreading "right-wing" conspiracies and Joe's famous Russian interference excuse.

(Remember, according to Hunter Biden's documents, 10% of all the monies Hunter received goes to the Big Guy.)

What was AG Barr's reason for not being forthcoming with the Biden criminal investigation? He claimed he didn't want to influence the presidential election. This is a bald-faced lie. His whole purpose was to influence the presidential election. He did influence the election in favor of Joe Biden and to the detriment of President Trump. AG William Barr's allegiance was not to the American people, nor to the President of the United States, with whom he swore an oath to uphold the law faithfully; it was to his fellow swamp rats.

With literal mountains of voter and election fraud evidence that consists of 1000 sworn affidavits, videos of election fraud in the State Farm complex, Dominion voting machine forensic analysis, and multiple calls to the FBI from US citizens, AG William Barr stated he doesn't see sufficient voter fraud to make any difference in the outcome of the 2020 Presidential election. Perhaps he meant to say he will not investigate any election fraud that could affect the 2020 Presidential election outcome. That, to me, would be closer to the truth.

AG William Barr earned the Helen Keller award from Gateway Pundit with his keen ability to ignore mountains of election and voter fraud evidence.

China Buys Influence in the US

Even more shocking is a leaked video made by a high-ranking college professor in China. He explained how they (the Chinese) buys influence from high-ranking officials in the United States and Wall Street. He complained that they (China) could NOT influence President Trump in disputes, but since Biden was elected, they expect more flexibility in the future. The speaker also inferred that they (CCP) helped finance the Biden foundation, to which his Chinese audience applauded.

Joe Biden started a foundation in 2017. It's first year, it raised 6.6 million dollars. Joe Biden suspended the operation of his Biden Foundation in April 2019 to focus on his Presidential Campaign. The Biden Foundation has been severely criticized for spending approximately two-thirds of its money on lavish executive salaries.

The video has been deleted off YouTube, no surprise there, but Tucker Carlson did a show segment on it and played the video for his audience.

You can still view the piece and the Chinese video on the Fox News website here:

[https://video.foxnews.com/v/6214769762001#sp=show-clips].

[https://www.foxnews.com/politics/biden-cancer-nonprofit-paid-its-top-execs-millions-it-spent-little-to-eradicate-cancer].

All the information that was being censored and falsely labeled by fact-checkers as false was accurate. The legacy and social media lied to the American people for months to protect the Biden campaign and help Joe Biden secure more votes to be elected.

Social media and legacy media censorship have been going on for years unchecked. They have censored positive information and pushed misinformation on President Trump from before his inauguration. President Trump exposed the fake news media, and now he is exposing the bias and censorship in social media.

They censor scientific information facts and push misinformation on the China Virus.

They censored pre-election information on the Biden family criminal investigations.

Currently, they censor posts completely or tag election fraud evidence posts as "misinformation" or "disputed."

China's Communist Party (CCP) influence in the United States should not be underestimated. They make considerable financial contributions to our top universities and colleges. These funds to our higher education institutes, I believe, are not without strings. They support flailing newspapers and the legacy media industry with millions of dollars in advertising. CCP appears to be intertwined in hi-tech social media platforms. As described at the beginning of the book, access to the vast Chinese market is worth hundreds of millions of dollars per year to various industries and markets. I have not investigated CCP's influence in the United States, but the little bit that I have seen certainly warrants a complete investigation.

I wonder if much of the censorship and bias I see happening with Google, YouTube, Facebook, and Twitter may be CCP related.

Facebook fact checker funded by China.

Source: [https://www.theepochtimes.com/facebook-fact-checker-funded-by-chinese-money-through-tiktok_3610009.html].

Censoring Evidence on Election and Voter Fraud

In addition to censoring information on the Scamdemic, COVID-19, Treatment Options, COVID-19 Vaccines, the legacy and social media giants are busy censoring all voter and election fraud evidence in the 2020 presidential election. The same people who lied to you for four years about President Trump, who created a pandemic from a virus with a better than 99% survival rate, encouraged everyone to give up their constitutional rights, stay home and follow every asinine government mandate, covered up Biden family crime investigations, now want you to believe there wasn't any voter or election fraud.

I've read all a fact-checker needs to do to delete or shadow-ban a post is to find a contradictory opinion or fact anywhere on the Internet. This can be from a radical far-left loony tune website anywhere, like CNN. This alternate universe information doesn't always work, as the fact-checkers found out when they fact-checked Candace Owens.

Candace Owens Sues Facebook's Politifact Fact Checkers & Wins

Candace Owens truthfully posted that Joe Biden was not the president-elect. Of course, this fact didn't fit the left's post-election narrative, so her post was labeled "false" and shadow-banned. Candace hired a few lawyers and challenged Facebook's Politfact fact-checkers. As Candace put it,

> Weeks ago, @Facebook censored a post of mine which truthfully stated that
> @JoeBiden is NOT the President-elect.
> So I got lawyers involved. Conclusion?
> @PolitiFact uncensored the post & admitted that they LIED by rating my post false.
> The fact-checkers are lying for Democrats.

Source: [https://twitter.com/RealCandaceO/status/1332711089604321286].

Source: [https://www.dailywire.com/news/candace-owens-challenges-fact-checker-and-wins].

FactCheckZuck.com

My Facebook posts have been censored, tagged, and I've been thrown off Facebook and other sites. I don't have the platform or finances to challenge these illegal dismissals. Candace Owens created the FactCheckZuck.Com website to secure donations to finance her legal challenges against the Facebook fact-checkers "Lead Stories" and USA Today. These fact-checkers wrongfully censored her posts regarding the China Virus, and she is challenging them in court.

I supported Candace Owens, and if you've been wrongfully censored, or do not like this communist-style hi-tech censorship that's being baked into all social media, consider supporting her.

Facebook's Post-Election "Emergency Change."

I believe my Facebook account was caught in this post-election emergency change. On Nov 3, the day of the election, both of my Facebook accounts were restricted. I was no longer able to post information or articles to groups. The New York Times reported the change was to limit news from mostly right-leaning sources. Or what Facebook likes to call it, "misinformation."

Source: [https://www.dailywire.com/news/report-facebook-used-secret-internal-ranking-of-news-sites-to-suppress-right-wing-sources-after-election].

Source: [https://www.nytimes.com/2020/11/24/technology/facebook-election-misinformation.html].

Facebook Injects 500 Million in Unconstitutional Grant Money to Tamper with the Presidential Election

The Amistad Project's attorney Phill Kline has brought lawsuits to different election offices across the country that accept millions of dollars from the 500 million dollars donated by Facebook to influence the November elections.

Source: [https://www.thegatewaypundit.com/2020/12/facebook-interfering-2020-election-millions-unconstitutional-grants-election-censorship-preventing-election-fraud-known].

Source: [https://www.thegatewaypundit.com/2020/12/breaking-attorney-phil-kline-expert-j-r-carlson-presser-wednesday-exposing-mark-zuckerbergs-dark-money-cash-chaos].

The Campaign Trail

President Trump held multiple rallies every day, leading up to the election. Tens of thousands of people attended these rallies. Trump's Oct 31 rally in PA, over 57,000 people showed up.

Source: [https://pjmedia.com/news-and-politics/rick-moran/2020/11/01/wow-massive-crowd-for-trump-rally-in-pennsylvania-floors-even-democrats-n1112834].

In contrast, Joe Biden hardly campaigned at all. He hid in his basement for most of the campaigning, and when he did venture out to have a rally, the number of people who attended his rally was an embarrassment. So much of an embarrassment that he wouldn't even attempt to have a large Trump-like rally. Joe Biden couldn't get more than a few hundred people at a time to attend his rallies.

Source: [https://www.thegatewaypundit.com/2020/11/freak-show-joe-bidens-final-rally-scranton-pa-tuesday-morning-awkward-empty-entire-campaign-video/].

Source: [https://www.thegatewaypundit.com/2020/11/call-bullhit-joe-biden-couldnt-get-10-people-campaign-rally-somehow-breaks-record-candidate-votes-us-history-no-way/].

Gateway Pundit reported that Joe Biden's Thanksgiving Day speech only had 1000 live stream viewers.

Source: [https://www.thegatewaypundit.com/2020/11/joe-biden-gets-1000-viewers-watch-thanksgiving-address-live-got-80-million-votes-hah-complete-joke/].

Yet, we are supposed to believe that Joe Biden got more votes than Trump. We are supposed to believe Joe Biden outperformed Hillary Clinton and Obama in votes.

16 of the 17 Bellwether counties that have accurately predicted the presidential winner went to Trump.

Source: [https://www.thegatewaypundit.com/2020/11/proof-fraud-16-17-bellwether-counties-went-trump-never-happened-36-years/].

Source: [https://www.theepochtimes.com/bellwether-counties-went-overwhelmingly-for-trump-in-2020_3579578.html].

The Immaculate Deception Report by Peter Navarro

Peter Navarro wrote a 36-page report on voting irregularities in the 2020 Presidential Election, titled: 'The Immaculate Deception.'

Source: [https://bannonswarroom.com/wp-content/uploads/2020/12/The-Immaculate-Deception-12.15.20-1.pdf].

Peter Navarro's document lists the numerous ways voter and election fraud were perpetrated in the 2020 Presidential Election. The Democrats cheated and got caught cheating; in every way conceivable way, cheating is possible. The topics in Navarro's document are; Outright Voter Fraud, Ballot Mishandling, Contestable Process Fouls, Equal Protection Clause Violations, 2020 Election Voting Machine Irregularities, Statistical Anomalies in the Six Battleground States, A State-By-State Analysis and Signal Failure of Our Legislative and Judicial Branches.

Each of the above topics is broken further down into topic subjects and then written on in greater detail. For instance, "Outright Voter Fraud" is not a singular topic; it is broken down into these sub-categories before being written on. Bribery, Fake Ballot Manufacturing & Destruction of Legal Cast Ballots, Indefinitely Confined Voter Abuses, Ineligible Voters and Voters Who Voted in Multiple States, Dead Voters, and Ghost Voters, Counting Ballots Multiple Times.

In each of these topics, the report shows sufficient illegal votes to overturn the election.

I hope the above shows the detail and comprehensiveness of this report and encourages you to download the report and read it. The report is free and is available for download using the link.

Source: [https://bannonswarroom.com/wp-content/uploads/2020/12/The-Immaculate-Deception-12.15.20-1.pdf].

This Epoch Times article provides a synopsis of the information, including charts taken from the 36-page report.

Source: [https://www.theepochtimes.com/peter-navarro-issues-report-on-voting-irregularities-the-emperor-in-the-election-has-no-clothes_3622874.html].

Hi-tech's social media platforms and legacy media are censoring this information. This is a cover-up! A cover-up that couldn't have happened without the help of the Republican establishment, DOJ, and FBI.

Dominion Voting Machine Weighting

Unfortunately, I don't believe any single report can detail every election fraud uncovered. I feel a comprehensive analysis of all the election fraud would be near impossible, considering the massive amount of fraud. One item (I think) missed in the report is on voting machine weighting. Weighting is a test where a Dominion Voting machine counts an equal number of ballots for President Trump and Joe Biden. When this test was performed, the Dominion voting machine reported a 26% win for Joe Biden. How could this be? When an equal number of ballots are entered for both candidates, yet one tallies more than the other is called weighing. The Dominion voting machines can be programmed to weigh votes differently. It was apparent the Trump votes are weighted less than the Biden votes!

Source: [https://newrightnetwork.com/2020/12/bombshell-georgia-dominion-voting-machine-shows-weighted-vote-counting.html/].

Source:
[https://www.americanthinker.com/blog/2020/11/when_computers_cheat_they_inevitably_leave_evidence_behind.html].

Source:
[https://www.youtube.com/watch?v=Ztu5Y5obWPk&feature=emb_logo].

Rudy Giuliani told a WABC audience that the Dominion voting machines gave a 2% to 5% weighted voting advantage to Joe Biden.

More Evidence

When false voter fraud allegations are made, if untrue, they dissipate and fade over time. When true allegations are made, evidence continues to accumulate. Such is the case with the claims of a rigged stolen 2020 presidential election. The evidence continues to snowball with videos, witnesses, ballots, and voter machine manipulations.

How can Trump supporters say there is an avalanche of evidence while the legacy media and social media continue to declare no evidence. Rudy Giuliani has over 1000 affidavits from people across the six battleground states that witnessed voter and election fraud.

If you don't know, a sworn affidavit is a written statement taken under oath to tell the truth. It is the same as giving oral testimony in a court of law under oath. It carries the same penalty of perjury for lying, which is, a person convicted of perjury may be sentenced to five years in federal prison.

The Left's Hypocrisy

In attacking President Trump, a single anonymous whistleblower had been given front-page headlines for weeks and used by the democrats to try to impeach President Trump. That's one anonymous whistleblower, but over 1000 honest American citizens who identify themselves and give sworn testimony to the voter and election fraud they encountered and witnessed in this presidential election are treated by the democrats, legacy media, and social media as liars.

The Democrats Believe One Anonymous Source is Enough to Impeach A President, But 1000 Sworn Affidavits From Honest Identified Americans Of Election Fraud Doesn't Warrant An Investigation!

In the media, 1000 affidavits from law-abiding Americans who eye-witnessed election and voter fraud are dismissed as no evidence.

Why aren't 1000 affidavits from Americans eye-witnessing election and voter fraud evidence?

On social media, posts showing evidence are tagged as being "disputed." This even extends to posts that are just showing the filing of lawsuits filed in US courts is labeled disputed. Really?

Trump's Election Numbers

President Trump received 12 million more votes in this election than in 2016. In total, Trump received more legitimate votes than any previous presidential candidate.

These 12 million additional votes created a problem for the Democrat cheaters. They had not anticipated that many more votes. To win, they needed to manufacture millions of fraudulent ballots and votes for Biden. You can't manufacturer millions of votes in a short period of time without being caught, and they were caught.

More Evidence Than Can Be Practically Presented

Like the Trump lawyers, whose issue is not having evidence to present, but having too much evidence from each battleground state to show correctly. A book can be written for each state on the massive voter fraud that is being alleged. I can only provide highlights.

New evidence is uncovered daily.

Multiple eyewitnesses sworn testimony of ballots being opened, filled out, and sealed in the back of vans.

Source: [https://www.theepochtimes.com/whistleblower-saw-people-in-biden-van-opening-filling-and-sealing-nevada-ballots-trump-campaign-claims_3570956.html].

Unmarked vans were arriving with buckets of ballots.

Source: [https://www.theepochtimes.com/tens-of-thousands-of-unsealed-ballots-arrived-in-michigan-county-all-for-democrats-lawsuit_3571675.html].

A U.S. Postal truck driver subcontractor, Jesse Morgan, confessed to driving 144,000 to 288,000 ballots from Bethpage NY to Lancaster, PA. Other eyewitnesses to pristine, un-creased (never mailed) ballots being tabulated.

Source: [https://pjmedia.com/election/tyler-o-neil/2020/12/01/whistleblower-i-drove-thousands-of-ballots-from-new-york-to-pennsylvania-n1184008].

Massive Early Morning Joe Biden Voter Dumps

What triggered the ongoing question of election integrity? Simple. Mysteriously after midnight on election night, the vote counting was halted in six battleground states, Georgia, North Carolina, Nevada, Wisconsin, Michigan, and Pennsylvania. Trump was leading in these states by large margins.

Then a Biden miracle occurred, against statistical improbabilities, not only did Joe Biden overcome Donald Trump's lead to win, he did so in six battleground states. What are the odds of Joe Biden winning these four states?

Odds of a Biden Win 1:1,000,000,000,000,000^4

The odds of Joe Biden coming from behind and winning are one in a quadrillion to the fourth power. (1:1,000,000,000,000,000^4)

This is according to Dr. Cicchetti, a former professor at Harvard University's John Kennedy School of Government.

Source: [https://pjmedia.com/news-and-politics/matt-margolis/2020/12/08/expert-the-odds-of-biden-overcoming-trumps-lead-in-the-four-swing-states-is-less-than-one-in-a-quadrillion-n1198438].

Source: [https://www.bizpacreview.com/2020/12/09/statistician-in-2020-election-lawsuit-lays-out-chances-of-biden-winning-as-one-in-a-quadrillion-1003758/].

How do we know there was cheating? Unlike in fair elections, where you see voters count graphs that gradually move and change, you see sharp spikes in this election's vote count for Joe Biden. These are called voter dumps, where thousands of votes are injected into the count. These voter dumps were almost exclusively for Joe Biden. And son of a gun, these voter dumps occurred in these same six battleground states Joe was losing.

In Michigan, there was a voter dump of 138,000 votes for Joe Biden.

Source: [https://www.thegatewaypundit.com/2020/12/michigan-poll-watcher-says-witnessed-shady-4-ballot-dump-joe-biden-dollies-full-ballots-wheeled-video].

Source: [https://www.thegatewaypundit.com/2020/11/mit-phd-analysis-reveals-138000-votes-switched-trump-biden-michigan-must-see-video/].

In Pennsylvania, there was a single voter dump of 337,000 votes for Joe Biden. Over 90 minutes, voter dumps for Joe Biden totaled 600K votes.

Source: [https://spectator.org/pennsylvania-bombshell-biden-99-4-vs-trump-0-6/].

What's even more interesting is that PA sent only out about 1.8 million mail-in ballots, yet according to the PA official website, they counted 2.5 million mail-in ballots. When this raised a question of how PA counted more ballots than PA mailed out, the 2.5 million mail-in ballot count number disappeared off the website. Everyone still wants to know how PA counted 700,000 more ballots than they mailed out. PA officials have not responded to this inquiry.

Source: [https://spectator.org/pennsylvania-bombshell-biden-99-4-vs-trump-0-6/].

Source: [https://nationalfile.com/video-crowd-gasps-at-pa-hearing-after-learning-of-600k-vote-dump-for-biden-just-3k-for-trump/].

In Arizona, there was a 143,000 voter dump at 8 pm [source].

Source: [https://www.thegatewaypundit.com/2020/11/arizona-voter-fraud-witness-army-col-phil-waldron-confirms-dominion-communicating-frankfurt-election-day-video/].

Source: [https://seeingredaz.wordpress.com/2020/12/08/fbi-investigating-voter-data-theft-fraud-in-arizona/].

Arizona, there were 790,000 laundered votes.

Source: [https://www.thegatewaypundit.com/2020/12/numbers-dont-lie-data-scientists-break-voter-fraud-arizona-shocking-video/].

In Wisconsin, there was a 100,000 voter dump for Joe Biden.

Source: [https://thespectator.info/2020/11/04/voter-fraud-in-wisconsin-massive-dump-of-over-100000-ballots-for-biden-all-the-sudden-appear-overnight/].

In Georgia, there were numerous voter dumps for Joe Biden.

Georgia

Under the pretense of a water main at the State Farm Center, GOP poll observers were told to leave. That counting was stopped and would resume the next day. After everyone left, unobserved counting continued.

How do we know this? We have the surveillance video of the counting room in the State Farm Center in Fulton county. The video shows that after GOP poll observers left, and there were no witnesses, poll workers pulled out suitcase after suitcase of ballots hidden under a table. They dragged these suitcases full of ballots to their machines and began counting. This ballot-counting without supervision or observers is in defiance of election law. Watch the video yourself.

Surveillance Video

Election Fraud Exposed - Suitcases of Ballots

Source: [https://lbry.tv/@OppressedNews:e/Election-Fraud-Exposed---Suitcases-of-Ballots:f].

We can thank the excellent work of attorney Lin Wood who filed the lawsuit for the surveillance video of the counting room in the State Farm Center in Fulton county.

The water main break was a lie to get GOP observers and news people out of the room. The break turned out to be an overflowing urinal in another part of the stadium that did not affect the counting. The urinal was fixed, without a work order, simply by closing a water value to the urinal.

Georgia Secretary of State Brad Raffensperger downplayed the video saying nothing unusual is happening in the video. The officials "claim" poll observers were not told to leave. The GOP poll observers signed sworn affidavits to the fact that they were told by the poll workers the counting had stopped for the night and will resume in the morning and that they should leave. CNN reported that a water main break caused the counting to be halted and would continue the next day. Where did CNN get their information?

The poll workers involved in this illegal counting incident refuse to talk or be interviewed without a lawyer present.

The bottom line, the surveillance video has not been debunked. Not even close.

There was no observation and no chain of custody for these ballots. One poll counter can also be seen running the same batch of ballots through the machines more than once. In other words, Georgia Secretary of State Brad Raffensperger's position is don't believe you're lying eyes, instead, believe what I tell you.

Facebook labels shared Epoch Times video analysis of the surveillance video false.

Audio Available

UPDATE: 12–8–2020. A Zoom link to a meeting was sent to Gateway Pundit, where election official Ralph Jones told government officials they were closing down the counting at the State Farm Center between 10–11 pm. Listen to the Zoom meeting at the 28:00–28:23 minute mark. Here's the link:

[https://www.youtube.com/watch?v=GAkT8Klkf5s&feature=emb_logo].

If Youtube takes this video down, I have a copy I can upload.

182

I'm sure Georgia secretary of State Brad Raffensperger has a perfect explanation for this audio, which probably includes don't believe your lying ears.

Three Georgia Recounts, Same Election Results Lie

Georgia Secretary of State Brad Raffensperger (R) performed three "legal" recounts of the presidential election. In each recount, he certified Joe Biden, the winner.

No Signature Verification

In none of the recounts were signature verifications performed to removed fraudulent mail-in ballots. There was no attempt to remove multiple ballots signatures, dead people who voted ballots, out of state resident ballots, non-voters, or a host of other mail-in ballot frauds. Why?

In the first recount, they only permitted one GOP observer for every ten ballot counters. Why?

Both President Trump and Georgia State Governor Kemp requested a forensic analysis of the ballots and signature verification during the recounts. Georgia Secretary of State Brad Raffensperger refused. The Raffensperger recounts were designed to keep and count every illegal ballot cast from dead people, non-voters, as well as multiple and duplicate ballots.

The attorney Lin Wood needed to file another lawsuit to stop the destruction of evidence (mail-in envelopes and resetting Dominion voting machine) by election officials. Whether this evidence can be used in the future is not known.

Source: [https://www.thegatewaypundit.com/2020/11/breaking-georgia-update-judge-issues-restraining-order-10-days-preventing-defendants-destroying-erasing-dominion-voting-machines/]

Lawsuits to Stop the Destruction of Evidence.

Source: [https://www.thegatewaypundit.com/2020/11/breaking-georgia-update-judge-issues-restraining-order-10-days-preventing-defendants-destroying-erasing-dominion-voting-machines/].

Attorneys Lin Wood and Sidney Powell went to court to prevent the voting machines from being erased. The judge first blocked, then unblocked, then blocked again, giving the attorneys a temporary injunction preventing the state from erasing the voting machines' data.

And the Count Goes On.

I am reading on Dec 17, 2020, that Georgia is performing some form of signature verification. After three fraudulent recounts, I hold little trust that this is a legitimate signature verification process.

Michigan

It required multiple lawsuits to obtain permission to forensically analyze 22 Dominion voting machines in Michigan. This is the same county that caught flipping 6000 Trump votes for Biden.

12-4-2020, a lawsuit granted a forensic team, Allied Security Operations Group (ASOG), an 8-hour window to examine 22 Dominion voting machines.

12-6-2020, a team is allowed to make an image copy of the machine forensically. The image copy is examined off-site for the next 48 hours.

12-9-2020, **Michigan's Attorney General Dana Nessel and Secretary of State Jocelyn Benson petition the courts to block the forensic report on the Dominion voting machines from being disclosed.**

Notice, all the people in Michigan who are saying there is no voter fraud are filing court orders to prevent the release of evidence of voter fraud.

Dominion Machines Programmed For "Systemic" Fraud

12-14-2020 Information that voter fraud was detected on the Dominion machines had been leaked. This leak may have influenced the release of the forensic examination. It was revealed that these Dominion voting machines are supposed to have a maximum error rate of 0.008 %. The Dominion voting machines had a 68.05% error rate. What this did was allow the election officials to adjudicate the votes. When a ballot is in for adjudication, an election official reads the ballots then decides who gets the vote. This adjudication of votes is without observation or recorded in a log. So 68% of the votes were determined by election officials.

Source: [https://www.thegatewaypundit.com/2020/12/breaking-antrim-co-forensic-report-bombshell-reveals-dominion-machines-set-68-05-error-ratemeaning-68-05-ballots-sent-mass-adjudication-giving-individuals-ma].

Michigan's Attorney General Dana Nessel also sent out Cease and Desist Order to reporter Shane Trejo to Erase Video Showing Voter Fraud Training

Source: [https://www.thegatewaypundit.com/2020/11/huge-exclusive-michigan-ag-dana-nessel-sends-cease-desist-order-journalist-demanding-erase-detroitleaks-video-showing-voter-fraud-training-face-criminal-prosecution/].

On Nov 22, 2020, Gateway Pundit reported that AG Nessel threatened to criminally charge GOP state lawmakers who met with President Trump regarding election fraud.

Source: [https://www.thegatewaypundit.com/2020/11/crazed-vicious-michigan-ag-threatens-criminally-charge-gop-lawmakers-meeting-trump-stolen-election].

Attorney Matthew DePerno of the DePerno Law Firm, who requested the forensic examination of the Dominion voting machines, received a call from Michigan State Bar. The Michigan State Bar decided to open an investigation into a year-old case. A case that has no complaints filed, but they are requesting 6000 documents. DePerno believes this investigation is politically motivated by his legal work on the Dominion voting machines.

Newsmax reported the following:

> *"In Michigan, the Secretary of State has ordered deletion of e-poll books and other evidence and also has taken affirmative steps to seal forensic evidence regarding the flaws in the operation of Dominion machines from both the public and from legislators who need access to this information in order to perform their constitutional duty," Kline said. "This joins with the Michigan Attorney General threatening legislators with criminal investigation and*

possible prosecution if they disagree with her, and the Michigan Governor and other officials shutting down the peoples' house and preventing them from gathering today to perform their constitutional duty."

Source: [https://www.newsmax.com/t/newsmax/article/1001540/1].

10,000 Dead People voted in Michigan.

Source: [https://www.theepochtimes.com/10000-dead-people-returned-mail-in-ballots-in-michigan-analysis-shows_3573209.html].

Michigan Secretary of State Official caught on video tell volunteers to count multiple ballots with the same signature during an audit.

Source: [https://www.thegatewaypundit.com/2020/12/mi-sec-state-official-caught-video-telling-volunteers-count-multiple-ballots-signature-audit-votes-antrim-county].

Arizona

Data Scientists use Raw Voter Data To Show 790,000 Laundered Votes Injected Into Election

Source: [https://www.thegatewaypundit.com/2020/12/numbers-dont-lie-data-scientists-break-voter-fraud-arizona-shocking-video].

To Preserve the Integrity of the Election Fraud,

Maricopa County Defies Subpoena to Audit Dominion Voting Machine in Their Country

Source: [https://www.thegatewaypundit.com/2020/12/mi-sec-state-official-caught-video-telling-volunteers-count-multiple-ballots-signature-audit-votes-antrim-county/].

Rudy Giuliani stated, "The only reason you (Maricopa County) would be resisting our examining those machines is because you know you did something crooked." I agree.

What the Cyber Fraud Experts Say About Dominion Voter Spikes

Two high-level cybersecurity experts, Colonel Phil Waldron (ret), and Navid Keshavarz-Nia, who worked with and has advanced training from the DIA, CIA, NSA, and MIT, agree that the Dominion voting machines were not secure and not transparent.

Even the New York Times proclaimed Dr. Navid Keshavarz-Nia as brilliant and cheered his ability to detect fraud.

Dr. Navid Keshavarz-Nia's full sworn affidavit.

Highlights

Here are a few highlights from Dr. Navid Keshavarz-Nia's affidavit.

Dominion voting machines are easily hacked, as demonstrated in these videos:

[https://www.c-span.org/video/?463480-4/washington-journal-j-alex-halderman-discusses-election-security].

[https://www.youtube.com/watch?v=KmihqVmKGT4].

Dr. Navid Keshavarz-Nia expresses high confidence that in the 2020 Presidential election, hundreds of thousands of votes cast for President Trump were flipped to Vice President Biden.

The owners of the Dominion voting machine company are not known.

The Dominion voting machines were connected to the Internet and could therefore have remote access to influence votes. The voter spikes in the battleground states late in the night are a strong indicator of voter fraud. In many cases, the voter dumps exceeded the Dominion voting machine's ability to count that many votes in the time period indicated.

On Dec 10, a featured article in Epoch Times showed how easily votes could be changed using the Dominion voting machines through adjudication.

Source: [https://www.theepochtimes.com/election-supervisor-shows-on-video-how-dominion-software-allows-changing-adding-votes_3613406.html?utm_source=news&utm_medium=email&utm_campaign=breaking-2020-12-10-6].

The article featured a YouTube video URL where an election supervisor demonstrated altering ballots and votes in the Dominion voting machine.

[https://www.youtube.com/watch?v=ijjwS6h-PyU&feature=youtu.be].

The Bum's Rush for Joe Biden's Presidency

Think of their quick 'bum's rush' to call Joe Biden the president-elect, despite on-going legal challenges in the battleground states. The bum's rush continues by the legacy media claiming the presidential electoral votes need to be certified in early December. No, that's not true. The real deadline is Jan 6, 2021.

Election Fraud: 19 US States Sues Pennsylvania, Georgia, Michigan, and Wisconsin

Just before midnight on Monday 12–7–2020, The State of Texas filed a lawsuit in the US Supreme Court challenging the changed election procedures used in Pennsylvania, Georgia, Michigan, and Wisconsin. The standing for the case is that these procedural changes violated the Constitution.

Soon after, 18 US States joined the lawsuit

President Trump also signaled that he or his legal team with be intervening in this lawsuit. The PA legislation also decided to intervene and joined the case.

The changes in these states' voting rules were made through executive actions of elected officials. The proper constitutional method to change election rules is through the state legislatures.

Unconstitutional voter rule changes have been a long-standing argument made by Trump's lawyers in these battleground states. Also, Trump's lawyers argued that there were differences in voting rules and procedures used in different parts of the state. One rule for democratic areas, and stricter rules for republican areas.

Massive Voter Fraud

While the lawsuit brought forward by the states does not mention voter fraud, it is because of the massive voter fraud that the case was brought. The massive voter fraud and evidence of voter fraud are apparent to everyone except the legacy media, social media, and Democratic party.

Censorship of the evidence in the legacy and social media doesn't eliminate the evidence; it only makes their consumers ignorant and arrogant in their ignorance.

The Texas lawsuit states:

> *Certain officials in the Defendant States presented the pandemic as the justification for ignoring state laws regarding absentee and mail-in voting. The Defendant States flooded their citizenry with tens of millions of ballot applications and ballots in derogation of statutory controls as to how they are lawfully received, evaluated, and counted. Whether well-intentioned or not, these unconstitutional acts had the same uniform effect — they made the 2020 election less secure in the Defendant States. Those changes are inconsistent with relevant state laws and were made by non-legislative entities, without any consent by the state legislatures. The acts of these officials thus directly violated the Constitution.*

> *This case presents a question of law: Did the Defendant States violate the Electors Clause by taking non-legislative actions to change the election rules that would govern the appointment of presidential electors? These non-legislative changes to the Defendant States' election laws facilitated the casting and counting of ballots in violation of state law, which, in turn, violated the Electors Clause of Article II, Section 1, Clause 2 of the US Constitution. By these*

unlawful acts, the Defendant States have not only tainted the integrity of their own citizens' vote, but their actions have also debased the votes of citizens in Plaintiff State and other States that remained loyal to the Constitution.

Source: [https://www.texasattorneygeneral.gov/sites/default/files/images/admin/2020/Press/SCOTUSFiling.pdf].

SCOTUS Abdicates Their Responsibility.

The Supreme Court of The United States refused to hear the Texas case. Their reason;

> *"The State of Texas's motion for leave to file a bill of complaint is denied for lack of standing under Article III of the Constitution," the Supreme Court's order reads. "Texas has not demonstrated a judicially cognizable interest in the manner in which another State conducts its elections. All other pending motions are dismissed as moot."*

In my opinion, this is nonsense. The Supreme Court of The United States abdicated its responsibility in the most important constitutional case brought before the court in our country's history.

SCOTUS shameful evaded their responsibility. Texas does have standing because a fraudulent election in Pennsylvania creates fraudulent Pennsylvania electors. Those fraudulent electors affect the entire electoral process of selecting the president of the United States. If that isn't "*a judicially cognizable interest*," then what is?

I'm not a lawyer, and I can figure that out. I would expect that the 20 state attorney generals who signed onto this case would not have done so if there were no standing.

The court's abdication of responsibility has been the challenge for the Trump legal team. It's not that they don't have evidence of election fraud; the SCOTUS and various lower state courts evade their responsibility.

Conclusion - Trump's Legal Team Lawyer Said It Best

To this day, 'our evidence has never been refuted, only ignored.' Why is Google so afraid of the truth? #BigBrother," lawyer Jesse Binnall wrote on Twitter.

The Trump legal team is fighting a coordinated effort between media, democrats, and establishment republicans to legitimize a fraudulent election. The evidential material present in this article is a fraction of the evidence. It's impossible to quote the testimony of those 1000 affidavits, stolen USB drives, and a host of other mail-in ballot voter fraud shenanigans.

The legal battle continues. The Trump legal team is currently focused on exposing the fraudulent Dominion Voting machines used in the battleground states. The Trump team is trying to obtain access to the Dominion voting machines for forensic analysis. The Democrats are blocking forensic examination of the Dominion voting machines.

The 22 Dominion Voting machines that were analyzed in MI produced fraudulent votes and tallies. There are thousands of Dominion machines used in the battleground states.

January 6, 2021, Contesting the Electoral Votes

A scheduled vote on the Electoral College on Jan. 6, 2021. Senators and representatives will attempt to block presidential electors from contested states during the Electoral College vote count.

A fraudulent and rigged election cannot be allowed to stand. If it does, it will undermine our US Constitution and Republic for generations.

Tobacco Smoke Enema Kit

Below is a picture of a tobacco smoke enema kit from the early 1800s. The equipment injected tobacco smoke into the rectum of a drowning victim. The idea was that the tobacco smoke's stimulating effects in the rectum would help revive the drowning victim. The picture shows the ivory rectal tubes and the bellows for injecting the smoke. Physicians began to doubt the effectiveness of the smoke enema, and this led to the famous phrase "blowing smoke up your ass."

This device is still actively employed by the fake news mainstream media and Democrat politicians.

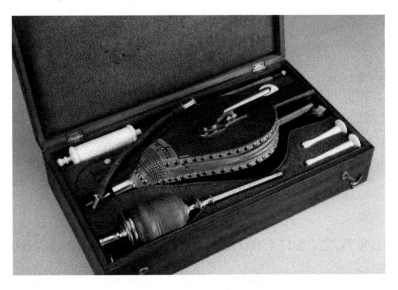

Resuscitation set, Europe, 1801-1850. Credit: Science Museum, London. Attribution 4.0 International (CC BY 4.0)

CPSIA information can be obtained
at www.ICGtesting.com
Printed in the USA
BVHW092146220221
600778BV00008B/1058